I0616229

Naturally Divergent

Calial McCarty

Copyright © 2025 by Calial McCarty
All rights reserved.

Printed in the United States of America
First edition: September, 2025

Print ISBN: 979-8-218-72438-2

No part of this publication may be reproduced, distributed, or transmitted in any form or by any means, including photocopying, recording, or other electronic or mechanical methods, without the prior written permission of the publisher, except in the case of brief quotations used in reviews, educational settings, or scholarly articles, and with proper citation.

This book is for informational and educational purposes only. It is not intended to diagnose or treat any medical, psychological, or developmental condition. Readers are encouraged to consult licensed professionals for personal health concerns or diagnosis.

All stories, case examples, and client references have been anonymized or altered to protect privacy and confidentiality.

For permission requests, contact the publisher at:
calial@mccartytherapysolutions.com

Cover design by GetCovers
Edited by Jocelyn Lindsay

Contents

Naturally Grateful

This book firstly is for my kids; I would not have been able to find myself without you.

You made me see myself as the beautiful autistic person that I am and in a way I would never have been able to, without you. You are the reason I keep fighting, advocating and learning each day with the goal of a better world and community; my hope is that you don't have to endure what I did, and if you do, then may it be but a fraction.

Secondly, to my husband who endured me during the creation of this book, while I continued a full client case load, and began my time as an adjunct professor. We continue forward in our life journey together and it only gets better and better each day. Remember that no matter what part you play, it is always important, and you mean the world to all of us. Thank you for being my rock. This book wouldn't exist without you.

Third, to the autistic authors who have paved the way for me to feel comfortable sharing my story and creating this book as a resource for others. I have learned more from your books, resources, and lived experience than any degree, class, or training could provide me (sorry, WPS).

Lastly, my clients! This is for you, with you and because of you. Much of the information in here, whether anecdotal or research-based, came from instances where I learned from you, we were met with a roadblock, or we needed answers. Thank you for trusting me to be part of your journey; I won't ever be able to express how deeply honored I am that I am someone you trust as your mental health professional. Never in my wildest dreams did I think this was where I would be when I was just beginning in my first semester as a wide-eyed grad student.

Introduction

Naturally Exhausted

I wrote this book to help neurodivergent individuals learn more about themselves and to help neurotypicals gain insight into other brain types. I am also optimistic that parents and neurotypicals alike will find many tools within this book to assist in novel ways of engagement with other brain types without asking them to accommodate to social or societal demands.

I want to pose a cautionary note: while I am fair and understanding, I am also blunt. I have never been one to sugarcoat things, and I do not plan to start now in the writing of this book.

Throughout this book, you will hear me use a variety of terms and acronyms that are widely used in the home, clinical, and school settings of neurodivergent individuals. There is an appendix with a glossary of terms, a resource guide, and other helpful tools at the back to provide extra guidance and examples. These resources are provided to help accelerate your use of the material.

You will also hear me refer to the population this book is written about in various ways. I will use person first language, as well as use "person with autism."

This book is written for many neurodivergent brain types in addition to autism, so references beyond autism are recognized by referencing neurodivergent student, individual, person and child. It is written like this to ensure that anyone reading this book feels they have representation and to make sure that all references to individuals are respected. It is important to remember that everyone likes to use different person reference languages.

I personally prefer person first language, but it is important to recognize that for many valid reasons, that is not everyone's choice. When it comes to everyday life and not book references, I encourage you to ask someone what their preference is and not assume, just as we do with everything else.

Writing this book was so important to me because many systemic entities continue to ask neurodivergent individuals to "fit in" with neurotypical society but never questions the societal expectations imposed upon someone who those expectations may not have their best interest at heart. It is never questioned if the expectations are reasonable for individuals, it is just required for people to blindly do these things because it is the way it has always been done. This should never be the leading reason a person is required to do something.

Historically, the responsibility has been placed on the autistic individual to endure the uncomfortable item, moment, or circumstance rather than the other way around. I find it important that neither divergent nor atypical neurotypes conform to each other, or do something that makes them feel uncomfortable, but rather co-exist together in harmony; celebrate our differences and continue to grow in unity. I understand that this is a dream at the moment, but for this to be a possibility, more education around neurodiversity, communication and socialization needs to be absorbed, understood, empathized with and put into practice.

In order for this to come to fruition, it begins with a further understanding of what it means when it is said that we need to improve the understanding of mental health and the use of neuro-affirming care. As the authors Fidler, Gould, and Wayland note in Navigating PDA in America (2024), the World Health Organization has a distinct definition of mental health. Time and time again, the medical model of mental health for neurodivergent individuals, as well as the school model (IDEA) fail to uphold the definition in its most literal form.

The WHO defines it as a state of complete mental, physical, and social well-being (WHO, 2023). It is important to remember that this explicitly means that being in a state of "wellness" cannot only be a liner model of a person's body being free of disease or chronic physical illness. What is also lost in translation by many professions is that mental health is not solely a state of being free of a DSM diagnosis such as bipolar, depression or schizophrenia.

You may have heard the same statistics on neurodivergent diagnostics time and time again; I am not here to regurgitate them to you. I am not here to pull you into the grasps of our world and send you into a dark web deep dive until the brisk hours of the morning. I am not here to bore you with the unfathomable truths around young suicides, and I am definitely not here to explain, at length, the number of teachers, therapist and other adults in positions of power who blatantly refuse comfort to kids who are neurodivergent just because it doesn't fit into their understanding of "normal."

No, I am not here to do that. I am not here to do that, because it has already been done. Time and time again, book after podcast after lecture after licensure, it has been done without drastic change in the people who work closest with kids.

Rather than move forward with the same information, expecting different results, I would like to leave the insanity behind. I see a chance for us to present different information, a different plan, and hypothesize, hope and expect different results. I see the potential for systems to reorganize themselves to be preventative rather than reactive, and to move away from the medical model, leave a reactive stance, and into a neuro-affirming structure.

If we don't look for communication, connection or collaboration, then we are not coming from a curious and affirming place.

Please keep in mind that this book is not a replacement for ongoing psychotherapy, psychological services, professional consultation, or any type of intervention for an individual or family. Rather, this is a resource that is to help you take information that you have previously received, or information you learn in this book and help you apply it in your everyday environments, such as home, work, school or community.

Within this material, you will also find a collection of lived experiences from myself, my family, and/or individuals that have trusted me to work with them as clients throughout the beginning of my professional career. The purpose of adding real stories to the clinical information provided is to give individuals validation in their own life, as well as uplifting tales of understanding; ideally sending messages to readers who may be seeking validation in their own feelings and wanting to verify that their experiences do not live in isolation.

These anecdotes can be a great way to apply learning throughout the book and give real-world examples to check for understanding. The identities of the clients in these stories have been kept anonymous, and some information has been changed to keep their information private.

Each and every person whose story I have chosen to share has read their portion before publication and has approved for sharing. Again, I want to thank those of you who have willingly shared your story for the good of the neurodiverse community, and for the hope that we can continue to connect through education and learn from each other as we strive for deeper understanding and better services.

Lastly, I want to acknowledge how complicated and difficult neurodivergence can be for a whole person, and that there is no way I would be able to cover the entire neurodivergent experience in this book. The number of factors that go into the entirety of a person's experience is immense and I want to say that just having that knowledge should be enough to provide a deeper and more empathetic understanding. Because of this, one of the appendices at the back of this book has topics that were not covered in this book, but are things a person may be experiencing.

There is no correct way to be autistic; there is no wrong way to be neurodiverse.

Temple Grandin said it best: "Once you have met one person with autism, you have met one person with autism."

Chapter 1
Naturally Diverse

"Diversity is not about how we differ.
Diversity is about embracing one another's uniqueness."
– Ola Joseph
(National Diversity Award Winner and Advocate)

Chapter Expectations

- Brain diversity is a result of natural genetic and DNA related variants

- Sometimes it can be easier to notice variants in others before ourselves

- Neurodiversity expands beyond a term

I didn't get an official diagnosis of Autism and ADHD until I was 31 years old. The only reason I began the diagnosis process was because of my kids. I'm aware my story isn't unique, as many others have begun their self-discovery this way. As a matter of fact, many of my own clients have gone through their diagnoses in this same fashion.

When my oldest son was 5 years old, I was in the assessment session filling out assessment history paperwork for the assessor. As my son was stacking Legos, the assessor cross-spoke to me from their vantage point, "You did a great job filling out the intake paperwork, thank you!"

I brushed off her comment and replied, "I'm a therapist and understand this type of paperwork."

"No," she said. "I mean describing his inner feelings and sensory needs. You must have such a good relationship and communication system at home, well done Mom!"

Now, I will say that we did, and do, have a great relationship, and for the most part a trustworthy communication system, however, I couldn't get her comment out of my head.

I spent the rest of that day, and the majority of the next, reflecting on why I was able to answer for my son's innermost thoughts and feelings. The only rational thing I could conclude was that I too endured many of those things and knew what the experience was like to the point where I had language for it and could describe it on paper.

Obviously, this then led to the conclusion that I was also diverse in my brain type, and it was time for me to begin my own exploration. Thus, my journey into neurodivergence began and I would find a path that led me right here to you.

Neurodiversity is not just a term; it's a perspective, it's a lens, it's a description of varying brain types. It views neurological differences as part of human diversity, and a natural human experience, rather than through a medical model, as deficits and as if it were a disorder to be cured. By focusing on this perspective, it shifts the focus from what is "normal" (as you get to know me through this book, you will learn, I hate that word), to what is "varied".

Neurodiverse brained individuals will process information, communicate, and socialize differently than what has been deemed as a baseline by the DSM-5. It is also important to understand that these differences enrich communities, workplaces, schools and homes. Neurodiversity includes many variations of the human experience and how the world is accessed.

In a world that continues to increase its understanding of the diverse ways in which human brains function, understanding neurodiversity is more crucial than ever before. Neurodiversity recognizes that neurological differences such as autism, ADHD, dyslexia, bipolar disorder, OCD, sensory processing disorder, Tourette syndrome and many others are natural variations of the human brain and human experience.

This chapter and the ones that follow provide neurotypical individuals with insights and strategies for neuro-affirming charged interactions that are meaningful and allow for connection, collaboration, and true communication. This is a guide to interacting with the intentionality of respectfully fostering an environment of acceptance and understanding without imposing or requiring change from the neurodivergent individual.

I am sure that many neurodivergent individuals find it confusing, as I do, that systemic systems such as academia and gender roles spend so much of their time and effort throughout childhood trying to force diversity out of us. However, as soon as a person hits the ripe age of seventeen, questions of the future are immediately thrust upon you from every direction.

A person can easily be shamed by various entities if they don't have an independent, unique, and diverse plan of how they want to lay out their plan for college, their career, and how they are going to produce 3.75 children all before the age of

28. In many ways, this explains a lot of the experiences one might have in society, and this is only one of the billions of interactions that a person has within their life. Hypocrisy is rich, isn't it?

A piece of my job that I really enjoy is discussing someone's brain type to them once they have completed an assessment with me. A tool I love using for all ages is the "cell phone discussion" to describe what it means to have differing neurotypes. I use this conversation to help people understand that there isn't anything bad about their neurotype, but why it is an important piece of information they'll want to know and all of the benefits to them knowing as well.

For instance, it's important to know when helping someone solve their phone problems if they have an Android or Apple (neurotype). Then it means that we now can figure out how to send text messages (communicate) , download apps (intake information), and what file codes to use (how to outsource information). I can be long-winded sometimes, so I am sparing you many of the details, but I think you understand my point.

Ultimately, I find that these conversations I have with kids, and honestly adult clients alike, end up being very validating. Sometimes, it is the first time someone has provided language for the things they have been thinking or feeling. Sometimes, it's the first time they have been given an understanding for reasons behind the behaviors they see themselves doing or, understanding why they have some of the internal thoughts that they do.

No matter what happens, I like to hit each one with a fun fact about themselves and why their brain is special and unique. An example of this would be: Did you know that when someone says you have "slow processing speed" what is really happening is not that you are a slow thinker, but that you have on average, 40,000 more neurons firing than a "neurotypical" brain type, and you have much more information to file through before you can get to the answer or information that you are trying to retrieve?

Again, the response is usually something about how validating that feels and how much that makes sense. A conversation follows, where they can pick out instances in their life that relate to this fun fact and when they think their brain was operating like this. I really do enjoy bringing relief and validation to individuals who have been discounted or discouraged at their attempts to "try harder" just because it isn't fitting into some type of "normal expectation".

Diversity within us is truly part of the human experience. As Tiffany Yu states in her book, The Anti-Ableist Manifesto, "being disabled is not the cause of our negative life experiences . . . instead it is the way our society is built to favor non-disabled people and discriminate against disabled people that causes us to be harmed."

Recognizing that there are multiple variations of brain types is an important step toward creating a collaborative and connective community. It is important that the notion that a brain is either neurotypical or not no longer defines the narrative. All brains are different, and all brains are beautiful.

Bringing It All Together

Key Takeaways

- Neurodiversity is a natural variation of the human brain, not a flaw.

- Differences in processing and communication are valid and valuable.

- Understanding your brain type allows you to thrive, not just survive.

- Tools like the "cell phone talk" can help explain brain differences with clarity and compassion.

Everyday Impact

- **For Parents:** You might see your child's behaviors through a new, more compassionate lens.

- **For Educators:** Your students may not be misbehaving, they may be operating with a different system.

- **For Neurodivergent Adults:** You are not broken. You just haven't been given the right language or framework—until now.

Let's Reflect

- Think of a time when you or someone close to you was expected to behave in a "normal" way. What would a more neuro-affirming approach have looked like?

- How might the "cell phone" analogy help you explain neurodiversity to someone in your life?

Chapter 2
Naturally Accommodated

"Accessibility allows us to tap into everyone's potential."
-Debra Ruh (Founder of Ruh Global IMPACT)

Chapter Expectations

- Why accommodations are important to each student

- A student's performance isn't always a choice

- The relationship you create with an individual is important

One evening, I was in session over telehealth with a student who attended a local middle school. We were going over what had changed at their latest meeting, as well as new IEP goals and accommodations. Preferential seating, check. Extended time on work, check. Class choice, check. Resource pages for tests, check. As you can imagine, the list goes on with other appropriate accommodations.

To be frank, the accommodations this student uses are necessary for almost any individual to do their best work. If you find yourself curious about what else might be helpful accommodations for a student, you can find a more extensive list as part of the appendix in the back of the book.

As my client and I were finishing up our session, I could sense they seemed disheartened. They didn't outright say it, but I had put together that they were feeling embarrassed by the number of accommodations listed for them.

I was conceptualizing that their emotion was coming from a place of hopelessness, as one perspective could be that they need too much help to be successful. As I noticed this, I began to self-disclose some of my own accommodation uses, as well as a discussion around the normalization of accommodations that we, as a society, do not have as often as we should.

I explained that the things listed for them to have access to their academic environment are things that each and every person does naturally in their daily activities. For instance, choosing where we sit or eating when our body tells us to is not an accommodation in our daily life, but rather seen as a choice of this or that.

Together, the client and I then proceeded with an activity where I asked them to talk through a normal Saturday that they spent at home and had them point out each time they did something that was on their accommodation list at school.

As they did this, it helped them feel more confident about their IEP and what they were asking from the school. They were able to see that they were merely asking for autonomy and communication.

Yes, I said it. Accommodations have turned into advocacy for students to have autonomy and communication. When we are at the point where therapists and parents must write bathroom access, water breaks, and food access on any kind of accommodation list, then that is what we are doing. At this point we are truly advocating for student autonomy back.

Another accommodation that is helpful is having a notes page on exams and tests. I understand that many teachers may find this to be controversial but hear me out before you write this off.

Students are in school to prepare them for adulthood and the potential for a career path in many cases. The testing procedure in schools has students required to do it all from memory, and if you don't know the answer, then the solution is to take your best guess. However, if we are to prepare these students for their future path, I am not sure where this practice would be acceptable anywhere other than the school system.

If I, as a therapist, don't know the answer or pieces of an answer for something, I say exactly that and I get to work on research or finding someone who does know the answer. Then and only then, do I provide an answer. In addition to that, I take the amount of time I need on assignments, also giving myself extensions if I need it.

I always sit where I want to whether it be a coffee shop, next to a friend, or on my couch with my cat, where I am currently writing this portion of my manuscript. I bring notes to sessions when I want to do a new activity with a client, or if I have very specific things I want to remember and need to articulate in a very specific way.

Could you imagine if your doctor practiced their job the way they expect grade students to take tests? That sounds like some scary medicine to me!

I believe it is time that we begin questioning school districts and academic establishments as to why they are asking things of students, and of course the population for whom this book is written for, neurodivergent individuals, to do things that are bad practices in any other environment outside of the academic establishment.

Aside from making sure that accommodations to the educational environment are made, there are many things that can be done intentionally in a school day to help neurodivergent individuals feel safe, happy, and even thrive.

First off, let's address that when we become neuro-affirming, just like anything else, we agree to unlearn bad habits, and open our mind to new things. This also means that we are opening our minds to the understanding that we may have been doing things wrong before, and that is okay.

You are here now to learn, practice and do better for the future, and that is what counts.

The mindset important to growth when wanting to become accommodating and inviting for neurodivergent individuals is a truly open one. Now, before you consider this to be anticlimactic, I promise there will be a dive into more specifics.

First, it begins with being open-minded. When we discuss being open-minded what that looks like is considering the why behind what is happening. Approaching a situation with curiosity rather than aggression or assumption is a key factor.

Many adults feel that youth make the choice to do poorly on an exam or engage in a specific behavior on purpose with ill intent; this is simply not the case. Many of the reasons for the "whys" behind the behaviors of neurodivergent youth in schools have to do with sensory discomfort, anxiety, depression, and trauma.

Extend treatment to individuals in a way that you would hope they treat you. It is important to reflect on if what you are asking of others, you would find fair for yourself.

For instance, if I asked my children to come to dinner "right now" but they are in the middle of something, they are not going to react in a very positive way.

If I, as an adult, were to reflect on a hypothetical situation of trying to type my thoughts down during a brain burst in this book, and someone dictated when I had to stop and pivot activities without my input or allowing me to find a stopping point, I also would not react favorably.

Here are instances where individuals who are in charge of providing directions or transition points can reflect on their delivery method and change the way they communicate so they are creating more of a trusting and collaborative space.

Instead, going back to the dinner table example, we could say, "dinner will be ready in 10 minutes, find a good stopping point and let's meet at the table!"

Finding out the "why" is one of the most important things you can do. No matter what your role is, parent, teacher or professional, communication, connection and collaboration will commonly be the answer in creating a trusting and understanding foundation.

Bringing It All Together

Key Takeaways

- Neurodiversity can cause frustrations at school

- Differences in the type of accommodations needed are valid

- Understanding your brain type can allow you to have insight into what may be the best approach to school for you

- Tools like "not spotlighting" or complete access to food/water/bathroom can be a game changer.

Everyday Impact

- **For Parents:** You might have to advocate hard to get these accommodations for your child.

- **For Educators:** Your students may not seem like they need these accommodations, despite the fact that they could be very beneficial.

- **For Neurodivergent Adults:** If you didn't have accommodations going through school and found it hard or you didn't like it, this could be one of the reasons why! If you are going to try academia in any form again, don't be shy about advocating for your own accommodations!

Let's Reflect

- Think of a time when you or someone close to you was having difficulties at school. What do you think their "why" was? What would a more neuro-affirming approach have looked like?

- What kind of accommodations do you think you would add to this person? What kind of accommodations would you have added to yourself when you went through school?

Chapter 3
Naturally Masking

"English is my 2nd language.
Autism is my first."
– Dani Bowman (Head of DaniMation Studios)

Chapter Expectations

- What masking means and how can this be harmful

- Why do neurodivergent people mask

- Masking can lead to wrong or no diagnosis

There was a period of time I had the pleasure of working for an organization that provided early education and intervention services. Here, I would provide assessments for children in their classroom and home settings when they were flagged by parents, teachers, or other professionals for appearing to have unmet needs.

One day, I received an email requesting that I provide an assessment for a student who had been having a really difficult time at home, but for some reason, they weren't seeing what the parent was seeing in the classroom.

Before going any further, I want to stop this story momentarily and point out that there are two thought parties many will divide into: 1. Readers who identify this as clearly a "parenting issue" and 2. Readers who are thinking, Oh my gosh, this is me!

If you have fallen into either of these camps, both of these divides will be addressed in this chapter, and you are most definitely in the right place!

Alright, back to the story.

Before I went to observe the student in person, I went and collected all the notes from the people involved. This included his teachers, occupational therapists, and family members.

Once this was complete, I went out to his classroom to do my assessment. His teachers reported that they truly didn't think this was about a diagnosis or behavior at all and believed this had to do with parenting or something at home. I took their input and then waited by the school's front door for the child and their parent to arrive.

When they arrived, it was clear that the child adored their parent and was looking at them for social cues and to complete their arrival routine. I made a quick note of this and moved on. Next, I watched as he ate breakfast with his class.

In my opinion, this was where things got interesting.

To accomplish his task of eating breakfast, his body posture was stiff in his chair as if his back was glued to a board. I noted that while he was sitting this way, he wouldn't allow his back to touch his chair. I began to notice a theme as he also wouldn't let his food touch either.

One by one, he ate cheerios from his spoon until the entire bowl of cereal was gone. Stimming, on point. Echolalia, on point. Sensory avoidance, on point. His masking, on point. Autistic milestones; exceeded.

What the teachers were unable to see, due to this student's high masking capabilities, which is why specialists are brought in, is that he was in need of help and his struggles at home were due to him exploding after a long day of trying his best to hold it together. It was apparent that he was masking many of his autistic traits, such as stimming, or facial expressions, while he was in his education setting.

What I was able to conclude from my observation was he was feeling the need to mask for a variety of reasons. It appeared that he didn't feel comfortable enough to unmask due to some specifics around communication, collaboration, and connections that weren't happening because the staff felt he didn't need it.

It is important to remember that a child doesn't need to be suffering loudly or disruptively in order to need better connections or collaboration. Many times, we see neurodivergent kids suffer silently because they are masking and don't want to draw attention to themselves, hence the initial masking.

When I took my observations and findings to the team of professionals, parents and teachers it seemed to be the missing piece to help them make progress forward.

The parents felt validated, and the teachers were able to use new skills such as communication, collaboration, and connection. At this point, it also took a lot of education around the student's needs and how they could help him as a team.

Approaches like this can be beneficial for families that find themselves noticing that their student is masking at school and then not at home, or vice versa. Not every individual notices they are masking, while others see how they are showing up in the world and make a purposeful choice to mask.

I don't know if everyone remembers the first time they noticed how they showed up in the world, but I remember mine very clearly. To be honest, it happened late in my childhood as I truly wasn't concerned with fitting in, I was unapologetically myself, until one day in the 6th grade.

Sixth grade was a year of major growth for me as I had some amazing teachers. Shout out to Mr. Liden and Mrs. Sherwood, wherever you are in the world today. However, that day I had a substitute teacher in Mrs. Sherwood's class.

One of the classes I had with her was language arts, and I'm sure no surprise to any of you reading this, writing was one of my favorite subjects. We were currently writing and putting these poetry books together as final projects, and I was quietly working on my book cover when the substitute came over to me and asked me if I needed to speak to the school counselor.

I know it seems like you missed something in the story, and that this came out of the blue. However, you are mistaken as you did not miss any context. This event happened in that moment then as random and without warning as the current recall of it. We are experiencing this confusion together, author and reader. It was that odd.

She didn't say hi, didn't come in with a beginning sentence, just straight to the point. Normally I appreciate a person who skips small talk, but this was a bit much even for me. Mind you, the only other interaction we had had all day was her calling attendance and butchering my name.

My response to her questioning my mental health was very uncertain to her—not because I was unsure I needed to see a counselor, but because I was caught so off guard.

She began to explain that she had read some of my writing and had been teaching for many years and knew that someone who writes like that cannot do so unless they have experienced unimaginable things. Here I am, no physical trauma to speak of, trying to explain to her that these stories just come into my head, and I like to write about them.

I am a little unclear of what happened next, but it wasn't easily dropped, and all I learned from it was that I was different and needed to begin learning how not to be different if I wanted to make sure something like that never happened again.

That truly was life-altering for me and demonstrated how others viewed me and my "talents." From that day forward, I masked, and I masked hard. It took me until I was 30 to begin my own journey of unmasking, and it is fascinating to me to think it all began in that one moment.

I am sure that many of you, neurodivergent or neurotypical, may be tired of hearing the word masking at this point. As I write this chapter, it is the end of 2024, and not only has this been a hot topic, but this word and/or topic has somehow been overused and understated all at the same time.

As a professional, I have heard the term masking used for a variety of things and not always referred to when talking about neurodivergent brains. Throughout all of the discussions, we have not placed enough emphasis on the biological piece that plays into masking as well.

Due to the different uses of the term masking, I would like to define what I mean by it, and how I will be continuously referring to it throughout the book.

Here, when I am discussing masking, I am talking about our biological and conscious, or unconscious, choices to suppress or conceal neurodivergent traits to fit in with perceived or expected social norms in a way to avoid judgment, exclusion, negative reactions, and possibly for survival.

The age at which masking begins has been disputed for some time now. Current research from behavior analysts discusses that masking is also biological and can begin as young as 3 years old (UC DAVIS, 2022). Masking can be something that a person chooses to do to try to "fit in" socially, or it can be an unconscious choice the body makes that tells us our survival rate is higher if we do this behavior instead of our natural one.

It is very important to note that masking does cause adverse outcomes in all neurodivergent brains and should be treated as any other "symptom" that needs support for a person to achieve their ultimate healthy self.

In the book Under the Radar by Dr. Emilia Misheva, she quotes another autistic individual, Joleen Stokmen, describing their own masking: "The way it felt when I had the last sparkle pony in a set—the click, the relief, the joy, that feeling of oneness, like all is right in the world. They couldn't see that. They couldn't see how hard I worked to be liked, to be like them. I turned myself inside out to be someone else, and I've paid the price ever since."

One day, I hope to be able to properly thank both of these individuals for this quote as it perfectly describes my own experience, and I am sure it does for many others as well. Remember that when we look at an individual who is masking, whether it's conscious or not, it means that there is something going on outside of them that is creating a space that they feel unable to be themselves.

It is important at that moment to do nothing else but look back at how you can provide communication and connection on a level they feel comfortable to help them begin unmasking around you.

In reference to the child from the beginning of the chapter, we discussed that he was masking many of his stimming needs as well as his other Autistic traits.

I want to end this chapter by providing a list of stimming actions you may see from an individual that should be seen as normal behavior and not attempted by anyone to be condoned, stopped, or stuffed down. When a person's need to stim is stopped, then you are stopping their body from regulating itself naturally.

We see stimming for many reasons, such as—but not limited to—happy feelings, regulating the body due to anxiety, and providing calming, repetitive motions.

Examples of stimming:

- Pacing

- Skin chewing/finger biting

- Clothing chewing/Hair chewing

- Finger taping

- Object fidgeting

- Daydreaming or Zoning out

- Coughing or clearing throat

- Smelling something

- Scratching/pulling skin

- Singing/listening same song/line/notes

- Watching same segment of video

- Cracking joints/big stretching

- Rocking body/bouncing body

- Leg bouncing

It is important to mention that not every neurodiverse person feels safe enough, wants to, or is able to unmask in their environments. I want to take a minute to validate that this is also ok, and every individual has to make a call on what works best for them.

The reason that we have to make masking a large discussion is that for the longest time the only option available was to mask. It needs to be a choice for all neurodiverse humans, not something they feel forced into.

No matter what choice you make, everyone should be respectful of it, as we need to assume you are making the right choice for you.

Bringing It All Together

Key Takeaways

- Masking can be something a person does consciously and subconsciously

- Masking can lead to someone not being diagnosed during an assessment and can lead to long-term harm, including other conditions i.e., anxiety, depression.

- Understanding the things you do to mask can be a key in unmasking

- Tools like recognizing masking behaviors in your loved ones can be so helpful.

Everyday Impact

- **For Parents:** You might see your child's behaviors through a new, more compassionate lens and catch new signs your child needs help

- **For Educators:** You may be able to spot and identify kids through a wider scope.

- **For Neurodivergent Adults:** Long-term masking leads to burnout, depression and anxiety. If this sounds like you, hopefully this can be a steppingstone to validation and recognition

Let's Reflect

- Think back to a time when you tried to hide the way you were feeling. What did it look like? How did it feel? What would it be like if you were doing something like that all the time, for everything?

- How can you help someone masking in your life? How can you create an environment that helps them feel like they can unmask?

Chapter 4
Naturally Autonomous

"All, everything that I understand,
I understand only because I love."
– Leo Tolstoy

Chapter Expectations

- Introduction to PDA

- Reasons that PDA is important to identify in a person

- PDA framework

It is common for a parent to come to me when they have reached the point where they have run out of resources, tried everything, or feel as though they are failing in their role. In all fairness, this is not just something that parents come into the therapy space with, this is a shared experience that I have had the pleasure of working through with teachers and administrators alike.

Each time this happens, I begin with assurance that they are not alone.

I, myself, have been in their position many times as a parent, school professional and community worker. It is important to point out, if you have ever found yourself being the one to seek help, no matter if it is professional or personal, then you are doing the right thing. Asking for help, especially when you feel defeated or at your worst, is such a hard thing to do.

When it comes to the topic of PDA, reaching out for help often leaves many individuals feeling discouraged. Many times, someone will have sought help from a professional, get tools with the promise they will work, and put blood, sweat, and tears into the application process, only to be met with that feeling of discouragement and failure once again.

One parent came to me completely distraught, as she had been to doctors, therapists, and other specialists, all telling her that if she was using the tools they gave her that they "should" be working.

All these professionals didn't know why the parent still experienced chaos on an unreal level daily, and they even began to blame the parent and question the child's level of services needed. The parent had reported that more than one of these professionals had blamed the parent and had outright said they must be "parenting poorly" if the strategies were not helping.

As this parent sat in my office, tearfully expressing her struggles to me, I couldn't help but think how sad it is that all these "professionals" continue to think that it's the parent's lack of follow through or ability to administer specific interventions that is causing their family such distress. When realistically, it's the professionals who are suggesting interventions that are not right for the cause.

We could sit here all day and argue about who is at fault but really what I see is a frustrated parent, a child who needs support, a child who still has many unmet needs, and plenty of interventions that we know are not working.

The parent continued to describe her child's behavior as the following:

- constantly objecting to demands/asks from parents of any kind

- hot and cold moods

- extreme mood swings

- using social strategies to avoid demands

- having extreme anxiety

This list of behaviors was not the only things that they described, but it did come up as their main concerns. For context, I find it important to report that this client ended up going through a full neuro-affirming assessment and had results indicating an Autism diagnosis and a PDA profile.

An instance where I see these symptoms, and these symptoms specifically in this context, most prevalent is working with autistic children who present with a PDA profile.

PDA, or Pathological Demand Avoidance, is a profile of autism that clinicians in America cannot diagnose through the DSM-5 yet, but as neuro-affirming providers we are trying our hardest to rally around that. In the meantime, we recognize it as a profile, and have specific interventions that can be provided to parents, teachers and other professionals.

I want to take a moment to say that I am purposely referring to PDA as Pathological Demand Avoidance, and not some of the other terms that you may have heard such as persistent drive for autonomy or pervasive drive for autonomy. I am doing this for numerous reasons, but firstly, I am following the PDAers/autistic voices and how they feel about the terms.

Secondly, I have taken my clinical experience, as well as consulting with other PDA/autistic expert clinicians who believe this to be the most accurate term description as well. In a discussion with bestselling author, therapist, assessor, and PDA/autistic individual, Lindsey Mackereth, MA, LPCC, LADC, we concluded that pathological demand avoidance was the best suited term and aligned due to personal and clinical factors.

Despite some autistic people who do not have PDA profiles saying that the words used to describe the profile appear offensive, many actual PDAers, including myself, will tell you that it does fit better and feels more validating.

Obviously, if you are a PDAer and you don't like the more common clinical term, you do not have to claim it, and we will not force you to (PDA joke intended).

Whether they are in the classroom or at home, the best description of the application of the strategies is as having structure and predictability without demands and rigidity. A PDA profile is a biological function in the body that constantly needs to protect the individual's autonomy.

The moment the person who has any experiences, or perceived experiences, that feels any threat to their autonomy, their fight, flight, fawn or freeze kicks in and their body does whatever it feels is necessary to regain their autonomy.

Once the individual feels that they are once again making their own choices within the safety of their predictable environment and the safety of their planned and usual structures, their nervous system regulates back down to baseline.

For those of you who have not encountered PDA yet, to truly know if you are working with someone who experiences the profile, it comes down to identifying if it is a pattern of behaviors where we see someone having strong or extreme reactions and resistance to demands, either realistic or self-perceived.

Something else that helps us decide that it is not a PDA profile is if the person is able to give someone control for praise but they can't to someone else. Another way is if they allow someone to help them achieve something based on a reward system.

Again, these are guidelines, and there are exceptions to the rules, but it would be rare that someone would be able to relinquish control or operate within a reward system if it meant giving up their autonomy.

To provide a quick summary, PDA describes an intense, passionate drive for autonomy and has a heightened sensitivity to demands that have a perceived threat to their autonomy.

Individuals that experience a PDA profile can find smaller everyday things like putting their shoes on, grocery shopping, or even eating lunch to be large triggers and can result in disproportionate emotional reactions.

PDA and all of the information/tactics can be very overwhelming, especially after I do a bit of my own info dumping on parents and professionals, so I have them leave the therapy space with a one liner (and lots of literature) to help them remember and gain confidence in themselves:

Calial's One Line Rule to PDA Success:

"Create Structure and Predictability without Demands and Rigidity."

PDA Traits and Key Factors to Understand

Sensory differences: Due to the extra-sensitive nervous system, they go into flight, fight, or freeze mode quickly.

Obsessive traits: Traditional supports usually make things worse (e.g., rewards, timers).

Focus more on details than the big picture: This is a space that allows the person to feel they gain safety and control.

Anxiety: PDA has many of its roots in anxiety.

Biological basis: PDA is a biological feature. The body is programmed to go into fight, flight, or freeze when it believes it is losing its ability to have autonomy.

Avoids tasks through social strategies: Due to high social acuity, they avoid tasks by using social interaction and identifying what avoidance is tolerated.

High-intensity masking: Masking helps them fit in and serves as a survival skill.

Triggered by praise or rewards: Rewards may feel like hidden demands or setups for failure.

Dislikes routine: PDA behaviors are not a choice to be oppositional.

Values collaboration and honesty: These are key tools for building trust and reducing anxiety.

For those adults who may feel like some of this information didn't apply to you, I want to give a quick adult example before I conclude this chapter.

Remember that when PDA is discussed, not only is it something a person is born with, but it doesn't go away. This means that adults with a PDA profile are just as prevalent as the number of children who have this specific profile.

As you read above, I am a PDAer and I would like to provide an example scenario to help give an idea of what it could look like as a person gets older.

So, there I was, grocery shopping with my children, husband and parents (which is unusual). I was in the fruit aisle getting everything we normally get when these amazing red grapes caught my eye. It's important for you as the reader to know, red grapes are one of my favorite foods, but they must be a very particular way. Super crunchy and no squish.

I went over to begin picking out my favorite ones, when my mom came over and says, "make sure you try one before you buy it, you don't want to get gross ones."

At this point I had been grocery shopping for myself for 15 years, and of course I try them before I buy them because I will only eat them if they are exactly a certain way. However, before I could control myself, I said, "I don't need to do that, it's fine", and I picked up the first bag I saw and threw them in the cart.

When I got home, excited to eat my grapes, I searched through the bags and grabbed them quickly; they were disgusting. I was so mad at myself for not testing them and for reacting in a way that only hurt me in the end.

In hindsight, this is something I recognize as a PDA response to my own parent, even as an adult. I had no control at that moment, and it tainted something I was looking forward to.

I don't always feel this out of control of my own demand avoidance, and there are many times where I feel it in my body, but I choose to not say it, or I can calm my reaction. Remember that if you experience things like this it is nothing to feel ashamed of and you are not alone.

Bringing It All Together

Key Takeaways

- PDA is a profile or subtype of Autism and does not exist on it's own.

- PDA is a biological base with a fight or flight response

- Understanding why it is important to identify a PDA profile

- Tools like the "one line rule" can help begin to create better communication.

Everyday Impact

- **For Parents:** You might see your child's behaviors through a new, more compassionate lens.

- **For Educators:** You may be able to broaden your scope of practice and create further trusted relationships.

- **For Neurodivergent Adults:** You may be able to identify this profile in yourself or others with this new information.

Let's Reflect

- Think of a time when someone made a choice for you. How did you react? How did it make you feel?

- How might the "one line rule" help you in current environments that you have frequent communication experiences?

Chapter 5

Naturally Communicative

"Communication works for those who work at it."
– John Powell

Chapter Expectations

- Become familiar with various communication types

- Understand why communication frameworks are so important

- Be able to identify other sources of communication than a person's "voice"

"They did it again," my client reported to me as we are in session discussing their week. They begin telling me about how their teacher continued to refuse to interact with them because they weren't using their "voice."

This client had been experiencing situational mutism for over five years, and despite continuing to work through different aspects of their anxiety, they had many environments where they needed to use communication assistance such as an AAC device for help.

When in my office, we used a system where I would speak and they would type back on a notepad, as their AAC device didn't have the flexibility to say everything they wanted. This worked for us, and we would also share things like videos and memes to help the client feel understood and validated.

Unfortunately, this was common for individuals, no matter your age, to have adults want children to "use your words" or "use your voice", but they used a device, body language and/or sign language, to convey their message to someone.

My therapy space is a safe place, and I explicitly state that all safe communication needs to be accepted, but unfortunately, this doesn't exist for many outside of those therapy spaces.

Aside from the conversation around all communication being acceptable, I also find a common conversation with families to be how to provide an open communication space for everyone. This can look different for many families, but for most it can be simplified by asking them to stay away from "no" answers.

Now, I am not part of that oldest millennial/youngest Gen X parenting movement where "we don't say "no" to our children" and they grow up thinking that what they want is given to them no matter what behavior they are displaying; this is different.

This approach to communication is an evidence-based conversation strategy that creates an open platform for all individuals involved in the conversation to feel safe and heard in conversations. In this practice, they also feel that they can continue the conversation no matter if the response they receive is negative or positive.

The traits of this type of conversation are important for a neurodivergent person due to the need to feel fully explained in their responses, heard and the want to ask clarifying questions.

Neuro-affirming communication is an approach that recognizes and respects the diverse ways individuals process information and express themselves, particularly those Autistic and ADHD individuals. The goal is to create a supportive environment that validates each person's unique communication style.

Listed below are six major keys that I deem unequivocally powerful in having a good connection and transparent communication with neurodivergent individuals.

Key #1. Understanding neurodiversity

Emphasizing that differences in neurological functioning are natural variations of the human experience rather than deficits.

Key #2. Active listening

Engaging fully with the speaker, demonstrating patience and allowing them to express their thoughts completely without interruption, or challenging.

Key #3. Clarity and Directness

Using clear, straightforward language while avoiding idioms and ambiguous phrases that may be confusing. Also saying the things that need to be said rather than expecting the person to "read between the lines."

Key #4. Sensory Awareness

Being mindful of sensory sensitivities and adjusting the communication environment. This can look like reducing the noise in the area or decreasing visual distractions.

Key #5. Empathy and Validation

As Dr. Bryson and Dr Siegel say it so well in The Whole-Brain Child, "Acknowledge the feelings and experiences of the individual first." This can foster a sense of belonging and acceptance.

Key #6. Flexibility in communication

Adapting communication methods to suit the preferences of the individual, whether that involves written communication, making sure they have visual supports or looking into alternative modalities such as AAC or PECS.

I am sure you are asking, "Why go through all the trouble of learning new communication strategies?" Or what benefit could this really bring?

I am so glad you asked!

Using these six keys fosters a safe environment for neurodiverse individuals to grow, learn, and have autonomy. It is so important to add that, when discussing communication methods, communication options like PECS or AACs—or any communication style that isn't someone's voice—always needs to be part of the conversation. Remember that when someone is using an alternative communication strategy, that it is treated the same as their voice.

Examples of this include never taking the device away from the person using it. The device/board isn't put out of the individual's reach; no one should turn down the volume without permission or limit the buttons or vocabulary they have access to. If any of these examples listed above happen, then their voice is being censored or taken away and that is simply unacceptable.

Unfortunately, sometimes, this happens in a school setting due to volume desires of the classroom or someone truly feels they are helping, but unless you have permission from the person that the communication device belongs to, none of those actions are acceptable, or allowed.

Listed below is a deeper dive into the main benefits that come from using these communications keys, and applying them into home, school, and community environments.

Benefits of Neuro-Affirming communication

1. **Enhanced Relationships:** Promotes trust and understanding between individuals, leading to stronger connections

2. **Increased Confidence:** Validating communication styles can empower neurodivergent individuals, to express themselves more freely and they may be willing to try more communication styles

3. **Better Outcomes:** Effective communication can lead to improved problem-solving and collaboration in various settings, including education and the workplace.

Neuro-affirming communication is essential for fostering inclusive environments where all individuals can thrive. By embracing and adapting to diverse communication styles, we can enhance understanding and collaboration across different neurotypes.

As you can see, there are many benefits to broadening communication styles. When these tactics are not used, neurodivergent individuals are left feeling invalidated, misunderstood, and shut down. Without these strategies, there is a loss of trust and respect between the neurodivergent individual and the person they are trying to communicate with. Much of my work begins at the root of families, and that begins with communication.

The moment we begin the "stay away from no" conversation and work from there, the changes in their home are incredible. The child gains confidence, the parents learn the information that the child was truly seeking, and in the end, the conversation ends with all parties feeling happy.

The reason we want to make sure we don't immediately say no when a child asks for something or asks to go somewhere, is because we are shutting the conversation down and not giving it anywhere else to go.

Instead, replace the 'no' answer with an answer that lets them know we can't do those things but allows the conversation to continue and let the child feel that they can ask questions or clarify information.

If the answer is going to be "no," make sure to provide an explanation that includes when they might be able to do it in the future and why it's not possible this time.

Moving from Closed to Open Conversations

Below are some examples of communication to help begin conversations and move away from closed responses.

Inquiry: *Can we go to the store?*
Closed example: We can't go; they aren't open.
Open example: Sure! Let's leave at 8:30 a.m. because they don't open until 9.

Inquiry: *I want that toy.*
Closed example: No, you can't have that.
Open example: We can't buy that today, but let's put it on your birthday list.

Inquiry: *Will you take me to school today?*
Closed example: No, I am going to be late for work.
Open example: If I take you today, I will be late for work. Can we make a plan for us to ride to school together tomorrow?

Bringing It All Together

Key Takeaways

- Neurodivergent individuals are great with communication when given the chance to choose their preferred type.

- Differences in desired communication types are valid and valuable.

- Understanding how you like to communicate best can be a great tool for yourself.

- Tools like the "open conversation style" can help families communicate better and can create a safer communication environment.

Everyday Impact

- **For Parents:** Your child will begin opening up and decrease their defensive communication styles.

- **For Educators:** By implementing these communication skills, you can create safe classrooms where students can create relationships and trust.

- **For Neurodivergent Adults:** It is never too late to try new communication styles!

Let's Reflect

- Think of someone you feel very comfortable and safe talking with. Why do you think you feel safe talking with them? What kinds of things do they do that make you feel so secure?

- What kinds of things do you think you do to make others feel safe communicating with you?

- Do you think you fit into the role of a person who would seem safe for a neurodivergent individual to have a conversation with? Why or why not? What do you think you need to change?

Chapter 6
Naturally Inclusive

"Diversity is being invited to the party,
inclusion is being asked to dance."
— Verna Myers (Author, Speaker, Advocate)

Chapter Expectations

- School models cannot meet the needs of some

- Dysregulation in the classroom

- Spotting a student in need

As I walk into the local coffee shop where I meet clients who are seeking meetings outside of my office, I see my client anxiously waiting for my arrival; papers laying all over the table scribbled with highlighter and red pen.

This meeting was specifically made to discuss their child's upcoming school meeting as this parent has been pushing to get their child moved from a 504 to an IEP.

Their child has been denied an IEP evaluation by the school team multiple times now, despite multiple state-qualifying diagnoses, and having below-grade-level academics.

Paper after paper, data point after data point, she had everything she needed to get an evaluation from the school for her child. Sadly, based on her past experiences, it didn't feel like enough.

We went over specific language she could use to hold them accountable for the acceptance of the information that this parent brought to the meeting, just to make sure she had enough to ensure they wouldn't turn her away.

This parent, just like so many other parents, felt as though the inclusivity factors of the schools, didn't take into account that inclusion without support and individualization only perpetuates more division and academic gaps.

The education system can be an amazing thing for the people it works for, less than fun for the people it doesn't fit well for, and a nightmare for the students it fails.

Now, I promise you, this is not a chapter about a failure of systems and the professionals that work in them, but it does need to be brought to light, that improvements can always be made and the failures do not always land with specific individuals or schools.

Sometimes it can be attributed to funding, resources, or truly just a lack of knowledge. Luckily, this can be adjusted just as easily as some of the parenting needs in the earlier chapters.

I choose to believe that the majority of people will always do their best with the knowledge they have; so, to the education we go.

Despite academic settings wanting to continue the inclusion model, the model doesn't always address the unmet needs that it creates for the students who are pushed into these classrooms. When working with neurodivergent kids in an inclusion model, whether they have an IEP, 504, or no legal accommodations, it is important to take these things into consideration.

- Dysregulation can be caused by large class sizes with both visual and auditory noise

- Dysregulation in general causes a major decrease in executive functioning skills

- Sensory overload, task overwhelm, and social exhaustion become more frequent, and it may lead to an increase in autistic shutdowns

- Students may need more time with materials before they feel comfortable using them for an activity

- Some days, even their accommodations may not fill their unmet needs, and they need other ideas due to fluctuation in skills

To close out this very short informational section on support for neurodivergent students in an inclusion school model, I want to bring up the dangers of reporting how well that "quiet" or "well-behaved" student is doing. It is important to remember that compliance is not consent, people pleasing is a maladaptive behavior for anxiety and many neurodivergent students indeed suffer in silence.

To help bridge the gap, professionals can begin questioning the behaviors of quiet work refusal, quiet attendance gaps, and compliance without fault, just as someone would address a student who displays noisy behaviors or aggressive behaviors. It is vital to understand that each person processes and displays their emotions differently, but that doesn't mean that there isn't an emotional experience or emotions are nonexistent.

As the theme of communication flows throughout, and the importance of connection and collaboration are proven, trust becomes a pillar that is especially important for individuals in the environments they find themselves spending the most time in.

When it comes to working with students who fly under the radar for a myriad of reasons, our first attempt at support should always be seeking out the students' perspective and gaining their trust. Engage with them and talk to them about possible unmet needs, no matter how they are performing academically or socially.

There are many tools that can be used to help foster this communication, but a large key is taking away barriers such as using the tool together, body doubling with the student, or using something like a communication sheet that has prompts for the student to follow to help the communication flow and topic generation.

When a child sees you on their side, focusing on their individual goals and capacity, you are boosting their self-confidence.

I have gotten to work in some amazing classrooms where these things were done, and the student-teacher relationships were what made the difference. School will get hard for every student at some point in their academic career; maybe you will be that person that is there to help them when the time is right.

Bringing It All Together

Key Takeaways

- Neurodiversity in the classroom looks different for each person.

- Sometimes a teacher can be a barrier to a student getting services outside of school.

- Aggressive behaviors are not the only signs of a struggling student.

- Teacher-Student connections can make all the difference for someone who finds themselves struggling.

Everyday Impact

- **For Parents:** Your child's school experience should not be based only on the teacher's report.

- **For Educators:** Your students can be struggling even if they are not disruptive and if they are following your rules, expectations and directions.

- **For Neurodivergent Adults:** These things can still apply to you, just in a workplace or community setting!

Let's Reflect

- Think of a time when you or someone close to you needed help in school. Did the help get arranged? What lengths had to be taken to get it?

- How can we begin finding help for those students who don't seek help loudly?

Chapter 7

Naturally Code-Switching

"As an autistic, I often feel forced to code-switch, to switch between two different types of behavior: my own and that which is socially desirable."
– Bianca Toeps (Author, Advocate)

Chapter Expectations

- Information on code-switching and root causes

- Intervention and support strategies

- Code-switching ramifications and importance of individualized care

A lovely family came to me reporting that they were noticing struggles in the classroom with their nine-year-old. The parents mentioned that they felt educated about many of the reasons their child was struggling, but there was something that they were puzzled by.

Teachers were reporting that despite academics being above grade level, and there being no "disruptive behaviors" to speak of, their child was choosing to not talk in classes, peer groups, or with the teacher. They reported that this had been happening on and off for a couple years and that they were worried their child was struggling with their mental health and wanted to find support.

When I first met the nine-year-old, they walked into my waiting room with their mom. They hadn't seen me yet as my office door is around the corner, so I witnessed a small interaction between the client and their mom before I met them.

They were discussing a game on the client's iPad and how well the client had been doing on it. There was glee and excitement in the client's voice, and engaging body positioning as they talked about this, and their mom was completely connected in the conversation adding the same amount of joy and excitement.

It was truly a pleasure to watch.

They spotted me and I stopped lurking; I really wasn't helping the rapport building part of my job by creeping my clients out during the only opportunity I had at a first impression. I introduced myself, and there was immediate silence from the client, so her mom took the lead and continued their introductions.

They both made their way into my room, sat and chatted for a bit.

I noted that only the mom was speaking, and then something magical happened. The mom and I agreed that she would leave the room, and I could play a game with the client alone to begin the important therapeutic part of building a trusting relationship.

The moment she left the room, the client was freely speaking, answering questions and begging to play my giant uno game.

Through building a relationship with this client, observing her, and reading through their assessments, I felt confident in concluding that she was experiencing something called code-switching.

Code-switching is when an individual is changing their communication style to fit the person or environment that they are navigating. When it relates specifically to Autism, code-switching also makes its way into skill sets of social dynamics and cultural styles. This is not usually a conscious choice on the individual's part, and they may not even know they are doing it. A lot of times this is something that can fall into autistic masking traits as well, as individuals are known to do this instinctually at times.

In the beginning of this chapter, when the client was with their mom, we can call that a singular code for the client. This is a program in their brain that instructs them on "this is how I talk, behave, and socialize with my mom".

Then when they began to learn about interacting and spending time with me, their brain was learning and writing a program, code or pattern recognition on "this is how I talk, behave and socialize with my therapist". Where it seemed like this student was struggling with code-switching specifically was in figuring out what to do when their brain was telling them to use two, or more, codes at once.

Some good examples of when the client is struggling to run more than one code at a time was when the client's mom and I were together trying to engage with her, or when she was at school and attempting to be in class having a group discussion with a teacher or classmates. It seems like her program "malfunctioned," and didn't know what to do.

Instead of her brain rerouting due to the malfunction, she had a type of meltdown where her brain found it easiest to not make a choice at all or possibly experienced a type of paralysis where she couldn't run the "right program."

Once I was able to gather all the information, I conceptualized that she was struggling with programs malfunctioning at school as well. I am sure she was having to flip through many codes throughout the day as there are close friends, peers, classmates and teachers. Each using different codes, many interacting simultaneously.

Between helping the client gain support for some of her unmet needs at school and giving her skills to work through these difficult social interactions in a way that she wanted, the client slowly gained confidence and was able to first begin talking and interacting with her mom and I at the same time. Slowly after that, she graduated to having small group discussions at school, and then continued to make progress from there.

It is immensely important to emphasize that during this neuro-affirming therapeutic approaches, never once was the client left out of the problem-solving process, and she was never asked to do something for the sake of "social expectations," it was purely based on her wants and goals; nothing more and nothing less.

Although this doesn't directly relate to code-switching, I want to bring up other important factors to neuro-affirming problem-solving processes that are important. When I say that we don't do things for "social norms" or "expectations," I mean this from the depths of my soul. Remember that not every person wants to constantly be surrounded by friends, not all people want to be the one to give an answer out loud in front of the whole class, and not everyone loves field trip days.

Some people like being on their own and find it quite soothing, some people don't like sharing that they have specific knowledge in front of others, and field trip days can mean you're being sent to a place you have never been before with unknown expectations and it's scary!

Like Stuart Duncan said, "Nobody thinks less of the penguin because it can not fly. It's simply a different kind of bird. Different. Not less."

It is here where we have to remember that all neurotypes are different. Not less, just different. However, it is in the face of difference that we have to remember that a blanket approach to something is not the right solution. Therefore, a solution needs to be tailored to the person that needs it.

In the case of this nine-year-old client, they most definitely ended up with a solution that was tailored to their needs, and they rocked it! It is amazing the strides we can make as people when we are heard, seen, and validated.

Bringing It All Together

Key Takeaways

- Code-switching is a common neurodivergent social masking trait.

- While seemingly harmless, code-switching can have serious long-term ramifications.

- When providing treatment or interventions, no one should be forced into something they wouldn't naturally or comfortably do.

- It is important to remember that the person and their needs are never a problem. Situational mutism is not a choice by the person, but the body's reaction to panic/anxiety/processing.

Everyday Impact

- **For Parents:** If your child is experiencing this, you are not alone.

- **For Educators:** If you have a student going through a similar situation the best thing you can do is provide a safe space and patience.

- **For Neurodivergent Adults:** If you experience this as an adult that is also ok! Many people also experience code-switching and situational mutism as an adult and you are not alone.

Let's Reflect

- Think of a time when you felt like you didn't fit in socially. How did it feel trying to communicate? What did you choose to do?

- How would you create a safe place for someone who was wanting to gain more confidence and become more comfortable like the case study above? What would you do to help her make progress in your classroom?

Chapter 8

Naturally Athletic

"Let me win. But if I cannot win,
let me be brave in the attempt."
— Special Olympics Oath

Chapter Expectations

- Knowledge surrounding why sports can be difficult for neurodivergent individuals

- In sport examples of struggles individuals face

- Tools for parents and coaches to make sports more accessible

I have many clients who choose to play sports, balance their academics and play a musical instrument all at the same time. A lot of our clinical work when this is the case ends up being around time management, burnout, and social dynamics, mostly with the adults they are having to interact with.

I truly believe that many neurotypical, not all of course, forget what it was like to be a student, or have a hard time having empathy for the student that is talking with them in the moment.

Students who come into my office to talk about altercations they have had with adults in their academic setting or sports setting usually tell me that they have little regard for the trouble the student is having, and do not provide empathy for the student's situation.

Now, before each and every one of you readers start to have thoughts about what the student did wrong to get themselves into this theoretical incident, that I haven't even explained yet, I would love to know how well you could see yourself as an adult managing a 35 hour school week, an instrument that is expected to have 10 hours plus of practice time a week, and a sport that has two-hour hour practices, five days a week, and games on the weekends.

I grew up around sports, playing sports and coaching my entire life. When my kids asked to play, I was on it!

My oldest wanted to play soccer and let me tell you, he was naturally talented and already understood game strategy at the mere age of 7. However, when it came time to do the sportsmanship ritual at the end of the game where you all gather-round, put your hands in, say a cheer for the other team and then go high five each individual person, my son completely refused. This was not out of character for him, as he doesn't like touching people he does know, let alone someone he doesn't know, and eye contact was something that was uncomfortable as well.

One day, we got home after the game, and he and I talked about the meaning of sportsmanship. I told him that as long as sportsmanship was shown, it didn't matter how it was done. Together we made cards he could hand to the other team's coach that had a message on it that explained his anxiety and distaste for the post game cheer, and that he wouldn't be at the end of the game high fives but that he wished them a good game and good luck.

In this moment I was proud of him for acknowledging a barrier to something he wanted to do and attempting to think outside of society's expectations and norms to find a solution. Neurodivergent kids run into barriers like this daily. It is up to us as adults to help them reach their potential and find those outside-the-box solutions that make them feel safe and seen.

Below is an example of the card we made that day together:

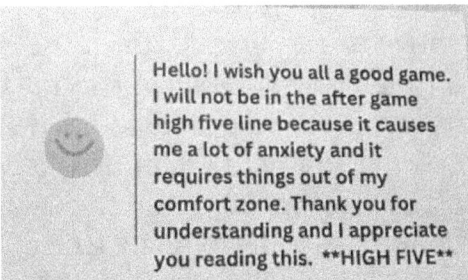

An important role in sports for a neurodivergent individual is the coach. By creating this resource, coaches now have more knowledge around affirming practices, environments, and coaching styles when it comes to their teams and other elements that surround sports. Hopefully, this results in making athletics more adaptive, accessible, safe, and inviting.

Sports can be very difficult for neurodivergent brains for many reasons. There are social cues involved, unspoken rules, rules that can change, things that are ok in athletics that aren't outside of the sports environment and in many instances, things happen fast. Very fast.

As I mentioned earlier, I grew up around sports, but I also played basketball specifically. Outside of my brain, I didn't move fast enough to truly hit my potential in skill, but in my brain, I was worlds ahead of everyone when it came to the intelligence of the game and what "should" happen in order for the most efficient scoring. I could be on the court, watch what was happening and be 10 steps ahead of everyone; however, to the outside world I was frozen, and everyone was yelling "Calial, MOVE!".

I had a very large brain-body disconnect and no matter what my brain was telling my body, it was defiant, refusing to move because the moment I moved, the game I was winning in my head was gone.

When I had to move or run up and down the court then I could no longer plan everyone's game in my head. Yes, I was telling everyone else what to do in my head, and it was glorious. Interestingly enough, I did find that when I played just for fun, such as a scrimmage, and the score truly didn't matter, I found myself capable of being free of this indefinite shackle that my brain barred me to.

Below is a starter strategy outline of action items that coaches can do to specifically increase their skills, as well as help families feel supported and foster a safe community for neurodivergent athletes:

#1. Speak with the family about their child's unique skills and worries

- **WHY:** This gives the family a safe space to openly talk about their child's needs.

- Coming into a new environment or team can cause a lot of anxiety for the athlete and hearing about them right away can be so helpful for all involved.

#2. Take out 'Punishments" from practice

- **WHY:** Neurodivergent brains are not motivated by punishments the same way as neurotypical people and this will create shame rather than motivation.

- If you need conditioning for your sport, simply involve it in fun games or explain that you are logically doing conditioning drills because the sport requires it.

#3. Provide "office hours" before or after practice for communication opportunities

- **WHY:** Understanding and clarification are a large part of success and trust, providing opportunities for them to know they can come to you is huge!

- Before practice the athlete can come to the coach and talk about something they didn't understand at the game and state why they made the choice they made.

#4. Take away Pressure and Demands

- **WHY:** Attempting to understand sports, rules, regulations and gain skills is difficult enough, but when adding something like "we have to win this game" or "only the best 5 play" makes that almost impossible or can lead to burn out. Don't get me wrong, I am as competitive as the next person and do believe that the people who have the best skills play, as well as the most dedicated players, however, this mentality has to come after the neurodivergent individual has the base skills and has been able to learn them without those pressures. We all know that recreational coach that goes too hard.

- We learn our skills and retain them best when we are without stress, and our body is not in a state of extreme worry or trauma. This also applies to sports as they are also a big game of muscle memory. It is hard for your muscles to learn new things or memorize athletic motions when you are holding stress in your core and other large muscles.

Bringing It All Together

Key Takeaways

- Neurodivergent individuals can struggle with some concepts within sports. That doesn't mean they don't like them or want to play.

- Differences in processing time can create struggles for players.

- Creating accommodations can help make sports feel more accessible.

- Parents and coaches can work together to help make it friendly for all brain types.

Everyday Impact

- **For Parents:** Your children may want to join extracurricular activities but feel it's unachievable.

- **For Educators:** You could be a valuable asset in giving helpful information on what the child likes best in the classroom for group activities like sports.

- **For Neurodivergent Adults:** This is something you could apply to a gym setting, or any group physical activity that you join in on.

Let's Reflect

- If you have a child, what do you think they would want to change about their most recent sports experience? Did they enjoy it?

- How might the accommodations listed above help someone you know join an activity they love?

Chapter 9

Naturally Anxious

"Worry often gives small things a big shadow."
– Swedish Proverb

Chapter Expectations

- Reasons the beginning of the school year can be hard for parents and kids

- Why teachers may not hear the full story

- What to do when hit with "every child does that"

I can't remember a time when the beginning of school was ever something that was looked forward to in a positive way. I have spoken with families where the child is looking forward to it because they are tired of the anxiety that is coming with the anticipation, and they just want it to be over with.

I have spoken with a parent who is ready for the break of having to do the full day by themselves, but I have never spoken with someone, in the neurodivergent population of course, who was genuinely excited because they love school (without any perfectionism attached to this statement), and just wanted to be there.

I personally despise the beginning of school.

I did as a child and now I do as an adult. School is a difficult topic for my own children, but for different reasons.

My oldest doesn't like school; it's fair though because the school's system, as I have said a bit now, isn't made for him. The system was made for the few, not the many. The school does well for the few children that can self-regulate, self-pace, self-initiate, and self-advocate. The number of children in the school system that can do all of those things is very small.

Something that is very hard for many parents of neurodivergent kids is the beginning of school, especially in the social media age. Social media can be hard on parents all the time, but really this is a place where it hits parents hard.

The first couple weeks of school, as all the local school districts stagger their start days, there are posts after posts of happy-looking children attending their first days and parents posting loving messages about their child's excitement, goals, and updates for the school year.

Then there we are.

The parents of those kids who have had multiple panic attacks just in the morning of the first day of school, let's not even start counting how many happened in the weeks leading up to this first day.

The parents who didn't even try to get a picture because that would just undo whatever positive work you did to get your child to the point that you finally got them out the door.

The parents who didn't battle what their child decided to walk out the door with. They might have a sweatshirt, they might not. They might have a backpack, they might not. Mine did not have a backpack. Mine still doesn't. I don't understand it. I don't think I will, and that's ok.

Whew, sorry, rant over! Let's move on.

Here...We...Go... Rest Easy, Heath Ledger

First, Parents I speak to you: Those social media posts are hard to see when you are isolated and struggling just to help your child transition to school. It is hard to see other people so happy sending their child to the same place you are forcing your child to go to.

We know the guilt you are experiencing as you are making your child miserable in the process, but you feel you have no choice. Please know, you are doing well with it. It is hard, and you are doing your best. Hopefully, we can continue to advocate for a better place to send them, and one day this conversation will not need to take up the space it currently does.

Teachers and administrators, it is your turn. First, I think it is important that you hear the struggle that the children and parents experience. Admittedly, you get a very watered-down version, and by the time the child gets to you at the school, the parent doesn't want to talk with you, they are way past overstimulation, and have to pass the child to you and run.

It's important to discuss that ultimately, school avoidance is not your fault. If it has gotten to the point where the child doesn't want to go at all and is advocating to be home, then it is so much more than the person leading the classroom.

A difficult part for many parents is when a teacher, administrator or school professional won't accept, or truly listen, to the reality of what parents are saying about their child.

I can't tell you how many times I have attempted to explain my youngest's behavior to school professionals and have been met with "every child does that, its ok!" or "I'm sure it's not THAT bad" or "I know they won't do that here, we will just see how it plays out".

The invalidation that parents receive from teachers when they are just trying to be open and begin the discussion is where some of the trauma begins for the parents.

I do not believe that invalidation is always intent on the teacher's part. It seems many responses are even coming out of an attempt at comfort and kindness. However, I bring this to attention for that exact reason. It is necessary that we begin to understand how to have better open communication around behaviors, and validating conversations with parents about the needs or unmet needs associated with their child.

Teachers, we want you to know that not all kids are like this. Our journey is unique, and the journey is hard. Please communicate with us like this is so.

Before I conclude, I do want to add a side note to this: When a school professional says "every child does this" or some version of this, I do believe that this may be their experience, and I don't think it is fair to invalidate this either.

An important piece to remember is even if the child is doing a behavior that you have seen from many others, the lens or root cause through which they experience these behaviors is what makes them unique and ultimately in need of other supports or interventions.

Bringing It All Together

Key Takeaways

- Beginning school is hard for parents of neurodiverse students.

- Parents struggle in their own way, they are trying their best and should be used as a valuable resource.

- Even if many children have similar behaviors, it is not due to the same root cause.

Everyday Impact

- **For Parents:** You are seen. You are doing a great job and it is hard!

- **For Educators:** If students do not demonstrate behaviors at school that parents report that is important information and should be part of the child's profile, not cause to dismiss a child's diagnosis or services.

- **For Neurodivergent Adults:** You might be having a hard time watching your child go through school in a similar way that you did. I know that's what got me!

Let's Reflect

- Think of a time when you hated a place you went to and had to go back. What place was it? How did you feel? What did you do when you had to go back?

- How might the information in this chapter change the way you approach the next start to a school year?

Chapter 10
Naturally Inspired

*"If your actions inspire others to dream more,
learn more, do more and become more, you are a leader."*
– John Quincy Adams (President of the United States)

Chapter Expectations

- Learn more about the author's background

- Gain insight into multiple-sensory loss

- Read about an example of communication differences and why it can be so important

This next piece has a special place in my heart as it really is my story of origin.

The people who know me well, know I love a good origin story, and are probably not surprised that I took the first opportunity I was presented, to write my own. Aside from the lightheartedness of this matter, I do feel that this next chapter is necessary to add, even though some of you readers may not feel that it is necessary to your own journey, training, or clinician research.

This is how I began, and I am certain I would not be here writing this book without this beautiful human.

It is important to me to tell the story of where I began, and who I began this journey with; I truly would not be the person I am today without them, nor do I think I would be a therapist if our paths hadn't crossed.

As I look back on my experience, I can pinpoint each extremely autistic moment of my own, each moment this child healed me, and each time we grew together. Yes, this story does also have information for parents, teachers and clinicians just like all other pieces of this book; this isn't purely reflective I promise. This might just be a chapter that you have to find your own takeaways rather than me providing a table.

It began when I had to drop out of college due to my inability to keep up and many other symptoms that I don't need to bore you with. I now know to attribute this to autistic burnout, however at the time I was simply uneducated and without support, so naturally I decided to find stress in a different antecedent. I declared to myself that society would expect me to find a job, so from there I blindly followed.

I knew I didn't want to work in retail any longer, as I had already dedicated five years to the glitter capital you may know as Michaels, and I was very good working with kids, so I headed to our local school district website to see what job openings were listed.

Lo and behold, there was a job open that matched a very special talent I had! What are the odds? There was an opening listed as a paraeducator in a deaf classroom.

Now, I applied as I was fluent in American Sign Language, but found it strange as I was very sure that our district did not have a full Deaf and Hard of Hearing program that was separate from other classrooms, but I wasn't going to argue with a job that seemed to be asking me to apply.

Fast forward to them offering me the job because there was a lot of back and forth before we got to my first day of work. The important thing is that my job ended up being something I did not sign up for!

I came to find out that I was in fact hired to be a one-to-one for a child with charge syndrome, autistic, and deaf blind. I was asked to start the first day of school with this student, no training, no information, and no rundown of what it means to be a one-to-one paraeducator.

What I began to observe day to day was how alike he and I were, how much I loved and cared for him, and how much he was teaching me about the world. The way he accessed his environment, and created a world that he enjoyed, is something I will always cherish. Some of my favorite times with him were when we got to find things that would create vibrations through the floor; things like drumming in music, basketball in PE or riding on the bus to a field trip.

Before this experience, I hadn't thought about what happens when you have a person who needs to access their environment differently.

This student taught me how despite him accessing it differently, it never took away from his experience. Many expect that if people are not doing the same things they are doing then they are not having "fun," but that couldn't be further from the truth. The reality is that everyone sees the world from a different lens, and that lens is beautiful. If we can take a minute to stop criticizing that lens and instead see what they are seeing, then we might learn something new about ourselves as well.

According to NCBI, it is estimated that 90% of autistic individuals reported issues with multiple sensory domains simultaneously. This can also be described as hyper or hypo reactivity (NCBI, 2020). This will be described in various ways for the individual, but it can be expected that they are accessing their environment in an altered way.

Whether that means that they are using touch to explore their materials instead of a visual examination, or maybe they are using another person to filter things for them before they go through the experience. The most important factor is that however a person is choosing to do it should never be considered less than.

While working with my student, his parent and I advocated for trainings I could attend to become a better teacher for him.

These training courses included the Open Hands Open Access training, focusing on communication with someone experiencing deaf/blindness. I was also able to access trainings around Applied Behavior Analysis which helped me understand behavior theory, despite my detest of it being used as an evidence-based practice for "behavior training". I also did my own research and began my long journey of ASD knowledge and the knowledge of what a person experiences when they have co-occurring disorders, such as this student with CHARGE syndrome and ASD as one level, and the other being multiple sensory loss blind/deafness.

Throughout my time with this student and his family, I also got to see the hardships they came across when it came to IEP meetings and obtaining services. Did you know that we had to fight the school district for me to keep my job? Yes, that's right, and not because they didn't think he needed the support, but because they were operating under the information that change would be good for him. Yes, I know the insanity that I am writing right now. I lived it and so did the family.

The student's mom had to bring research and information to the school to show that having consistency in his school accommodation was necessary for his academic access.

For reference, anyone who is wondering what year this was, it was 2015.

The parent won the fight, and I got to keep my job, but they still made me re-interview every year. It was insanity and caused me quite a bit of anxiety. When I tell you that student was worth it, I mean it with every fiber of my being.

While at this job, I began my own schooling again and went for my bachelor's degree in psychology of applied behavior analysis.

I don't want to spend much time on this, but I do want to clarify that the study of behavior analysis and behavior theory is not the same thing as the evidence-based practice of ABA therapy.

It was amazing going through school and in parallel going to work and doing things that were talked about but hands-on. I am so thankful that things played out that way as it is my best learning style, and I can't express how different a student I was because of it.

Thanks to him, every time I meet a client, I know connection is key and collaboration is a must as we need to see the world from their view as much as possible.

Bud, if you ever read this book, just know you are always on my mind and forever in my heart.

Bringing It All Together

Key Takeaways

- I would not have ended up where I am without this person.

- Differences in processing can also be connected to sensory processing.

- We are multidimensional and when we experience sensory loss, it can change the way we want to communicate or explore the environment.

- Each experience in life is full of things to learn from.

Everyday Impact

- **For Parents:** Your child will explore the world through their own sensory needs. Their way is their own and not wrong.

- **For Educators:** Allow students to explore their materials and spaces in their own way and in the amount of time they need.

- **For Neurodivergent Adults:** If you are not currently exploring things and environments the way you need to, use this to feel empowered to start now.

Let's Reflect

• Think of a time when you were unable to do something the way you wanted to. How did it feel? How do you think it changed the thing for you having to do it someone else's way?

• How might this information change the way you interact with others when it comes to working on things with them or coordinating with others?

Chapter 11
Naturally Literal

"I have autism, but autism doesn't have me."
– Henry Frost (Author, Advocate)

Chapter Expectations

- School Communication

- Intervention and support strategies

- Setting up expectations for best practices

Alright, enough about me, back to you, the reader, and of course: clients! Let's take this back to the office and back to another parent that found themselves struggling when it came to getting support for their child.

A parent came into session with me, sat down, and said, "Ok, it's your turn. I can't talk to them anymore! They aren't listening to me, and I am pretty sure they think I am crazy."

Of course, I already knew what she was referring to based on our previous conversations, but nevertheless, I asked for context.

She reported that she had gone to the school to speak with them about the behaviors her child had been demonstrating in class, such as work refusal, refusing to participate in class, and sometimes disrupting instruction time with loudly announcing he was leaving the classroom because he felt they "lied" to him. As the student would walk out of the classroom, he would continue the behavior by explaining, very clearly, that he felt "they were not doing what they said they would".

She said that when discussing the behaviors, the school described them as disruptive, and they needed to stop, but didn't offer any suggestions or even claim any responsibility as to why the behaviors were happening.

When I asked for the parent to describe what she felt were the reasons behind the behaviors that were happening, she was able to answer me without hesitation; "I think it has to do with him feeling 'tricked'." She said that she didn't know what to do and felt that the school didn't appear supportive in finding solutions, but rather just wanted it to be "fixed".

This mom reported she felt very unsure of how to communicate the needs of her child. I let her know that this was something we could figure out together and that she was not alone in this sentiment.

This is something that is a common conversation and it revolves around neurodivergent children feeling that expectations are not being laid out clearly, and they are being falsely led. There are also feelings that things are not being followed through in a way that feels fair to the child.

Many neurodivergent brain types also have a large sense of justice not just for others, but for themselves. When they feel an injustice is happening this can trigger a roadblock in the moment and could be a way a child loses respect and trust for the professionals in their school day.

Wonderful first steps to work through these difficult instances include coaching families through best ways to communicate what their child needs are to the teacher or professional. Once parents feel like the school professionals clearly understand that, then the team can move onto response strategies. These look like ways that the team should and shouldn't respond to the behavior, and why consistency is of the utmost importance.

This particularly comes up when a family is notified by the school that their student is showing what the school describes as "disruptive behaviors." Many times, the coping strategies that teachers have tried before contacting their parents are not coping strategies that match the student's brain type and are usually interventions that are more suited for a neurotypical brain style.

A very common situation where a neurodivergent neurotype finds themselves dysregulated is when there are no clear expectations being set up in the classroom. A good example of this can be the following:

A teacher says to the classroom, "What movie should we watch? I have Inside Out, Frozen and Toy Story."

The neurodivergent child in question screams with burning passion, "Toy Story!!!!"

As the discussion continues, the teacher sees that there is more overall classroom approval for the movie Inside Out; therefore, the teacher says, "Ok, thank you for all of your votes, we will watch Inside Out."

This statement sends the child into a very dysregulated, and angry state internally. He demonstrates this by externally screaming "NO!!!" and then continuing to stomp around the classroom demonstrating his anger very clearly and then proceeds to have a meltdown.

The problem with the way this hypothetical teacher went about this is they didn't explicitly state they were going to choose the movie with the most approval. They simply asked a question that suggested if the student were to answer it, then the answer would grant what the person wanted.

A way that someone could go about doing the same thing, but having different results, is to make sure that all expectations are set out before performing any actions. It needs to be clearly described to the class that the teacher had brought three movies as a choice for the group, and that the movie choice would be based on popular vote.

Saying something such as, "whichever movie has the most votes will be the movie chosen for us to watch," will be helpful. There is importance in creating a situation where the choice is quantifiable and will make sense to the child. It is logical, even if they are disappointed.

Other examples of good times to incorporate extra expectations in classroom settings can be in group projects, unstructured social time, specialist classes (e.g. physical education, library, music classes) and times where the student thrives like technology or art. Obviously, based on the student, their brain type, and the way they process information, the way expectations are set will be individualized, but here are some overarching examples that may help you feel like you have a good foundation to begin with.

Below are evidence-based accommodations that can be applied to most classrooms, and many situations where a neurodivergent brain type may be struggling in the classroom due to their unmet needs and possible misunderstanding of expectations. There are many other ways to accommodate, or accomplish what a student may need, but these are a few core accommodations that will give any teacher a great foundation to build from.

Educational Accommodation Strategies

Use the following strategies to better support students with unmet needs. Each includes the teacher's role, an example action, and why it helps.

#1. Adjust
Teacher Role: Make small adjustments to align with skills or unmet needs in the moment
Action Example: Point out the learner's key parts
Why This Helps: Students become less overwhelmed and gain confidence

#2. Communication
Teacher Role: Increase frequency and literalness in expectations that are set
Action Example: Check for understanding and allow for clarification questions
Why This Helps: When the student understands all details and outcomes, completing the task feels safer

#3. Time
Teacher Role: Modify time requirements to give more time and space
Action Example: Help identify if the unmet need falls into executive functioning, sensory, or learning differences
Why This Helps: Student has the time restraint lifted and support in the area they are struggling with

#4. Collaboration
Teacher Role: Decrease or eliminate power imbalances or power struggles
Action Example: Provide choice and control to the student
Why This Helps: This reduces anxiety for the student and allows them to be ready for problem-solving

#5. Social Support
Teacher Role: Get insight from parents, school team members, and therapists/doctors
Action Example: Discuss with parents strategies they see as most successful
Why This Helps: This highlights a whole-child approach

I understand that these accommodations listed are very bland and broad so I know that in each situation where a student is struggling, there will always need to be a more in-depth discussions within the student's team members.

As stated before, earlier in this chapter, many well intentioned interventions do not work well for neurodivergent students and can even, in some cases, make things worse.

Now, let's take a deeper dive into discussing why some of the first step accommodations that schools provide with good intentions may not be as helpful for a neurodivergent student.

One very common accommodation is "allowing breaks." Many schools, especially at the elementary stage, label it a "feelings corner" and have an entire curriculum around it. Many places encourage students to utilize this when needed, and they are even taught to go there when they are experiencing "big feelings."

An example of this would be our student that was referenced at the beginning of this chapter. The staff aspired to have him take a break when he was feeling frustrated or beginning to "flip his lid." However, a large barrier to this, as it is with many others, our student had a hard time identifying his own emotions, found difficulty being in touch with his interoceptive senses and scored significantly high on the alexithymic scale.

On top of the many reasons this can be a struggle and frustration when it comes to intervention strategies, this technique is also asking the student to catch their emotions at the proper time.

For instance, if we discussed that the student from above is not capable of self-identifying when he needs a break or he is rapidly changing emotionally, then it is again, something we can teach with the skills in the table.

First, providing language around this can look like the student leaving his space to go do his Legos, or whatever activity break that is provided for the student (i.e., fidgets, stuffies) and a teacher can approach him a couple minutes after he begins his activity and say out loud to the student "I saw you using the Legos, I wonder if something frustrated you?"

The idea surrounding this is after consistently completing this coping strategy with the language component paired, and the assistance from an adult to regulate his emotions and body, he will give an answer that will lead the staff to be able to continue the conversation.

The hope is that the answers will then lead to information for staff and other individuals in the direction of what will be the best next steps to help him and regulate his body; or the "why" to his dysregulation.

These truly are first steps in teaching conversations to help him begin to learn about his needs, body and emotions and how to self-identify in these situations.

If we can begin doing these things in the classrooms, at home and in the communities at young ages for kids, it can make a world of difference for how they see their own ability to communicate with others and represent themselves in conversation.

Teaching that collaboration is key will help build a solid foundation for difficult things they will come up against, and what an amazing feeling to be part of building a foundation like that for someone.

Bringing It All Together

Key Takeaways

- It is important to lay out all expectations from the beginning.

- If a student becomes emotional, do not react with punishment but name it what it is: a miscommunication; then treat it as such.

- Failing to set up rules and expectations can lead to students filling in details by assumptions.

- Tools like the "educational accommodations" can be helpful when beginning to laydown expectations.

Everyday Impact

- **For Parents**: This can create a good base framework to communicate with school staff.

- **For Educators:** Your students and you have a building point for rules and expectations to be laid out.

- **For Neurodivergent Adults:** This is also a great communication tool to start discussing other expectations. This can work for just talking about organizing a Friday night dinner out!

Let's Reflect

- Think of a time when you or someone close to you had a miscommunication around expectations. Did you find it frustrating? How did you fix it? Do you think your child/a child would be able to independently navigate that same situation that you were just thinking of?

- How might the "classroom accommodations" bring your own family assistance in the classroom?

Chapter 12
Naturally Traumatized

"Abuse is never deserved, it is an exploitation
of innocence and physical disadvantage,
which is perceived as an opportunity by the abuser."
– Lorraine Nilon (Survivor, Author)

Chapter Expectations

- Knowledge around co-occurrence between PTSD and other neurodivergence

- What a transition out of "freeze" response looks like

- The importance of skills for all individuals who are part of a team

I was brought onto a case where a client had been through an immense amount of trauma. I believe that in our world using a word like "situational" to describe a person's trauma is a way to relinquish the responsibility of the harm caused by the abuser. However, it is important to find a way to recognize that children who experience trauma literally have no control over it and no choice.

I am not speaking from a place of victim blaming or invalidating other trauma victims or the reasons that they also found themselves without a choice of enduring their own brutal experiences. I am also not stating that an individual has control over the trauma that they endure. What I want to simply point out is that with children the understanding that their trauma and situation is even more complex needs to be at the root of every discussion. Children do not have a choice. Children cannot leave even if they are aware enough to identify they are in an unsafe situation.

The reasoning behind my addition to the already stacked roster for the client had to do with his brain type and his selective speech. We hit the ground running and both his guardian and I were able to see him make leaps of progress in a short amount of time.

As I spent more time with the two of them, I was able to learn how he was doing at school, and what some of his unmet needs were. His family members were noticing that the combination of his CPTSD and other co-morbidities affected how he approached things and as the client became more comfortable in his surroundings. They began to see that it was no longer something they felt was due to an adjustment period and felt these symptoms were manifesting themselves in his everyday life and various environments.

As we continued our work in the therapy space and home environment, he continued to show improvements with opening up, emotional regulation and showing a wider range of emotions within his artwork. He began hitting some of these milestones after a couple of years of stabilization, development, and being in a safe environment.

During this time of progress, the family began receiving notes home from the client's school saying he would leave the classroom during a certain "loud noise" or something that the staff reported as an unknown reaction.

What the school was reporting as a problem—and I am sure they had safety at the forefront of their minds—was something that we celebrated!

As the clinician, I was so happy to see that my client was making progress. The progress I was seeing from him was he was no longer making the choice to mask or freeze through something causing his body a trauma response. He was no longer enduring external or internal stimuli that was disruptive or triggering to him, but rather listening to his instincts and interoceptive senses, all while acting in a way he felt would protect himself. Together, we saw this as the first steps in this child advocating for his needs in the way he was able to communicate it during that moment.

At this point, during someone's first steps in changes of their reactions, it's perfectly normal for the school and the family to hold a meeting to create some sort of plan to both help the student who is learning something new about themselves, as well as help guide them through doing it in a safe and affirming way. It is important to recognize that while having a plan set in place for a person can be helpful, the outcome of the plan is only as good as what it can provide when the person is dysregulated.

Many team members will want to say that it works during a child's baseline or regulated moments, which is much different than saying that it works, or is a good option when someone is dysregulated or experiencing symptoms related to their mental health needs and/or unmet needs.

Again, any time anyone wants to implement something new, it needs to be taught in multiple ways and practiced when the person is at baseline so that they can use it when they need it. When a person is dysregulated, especially someone who has CPTSD, their brain is shut down to discussion, learning or outside sources when their body is triggered.

A recurrent and hot topic in the autistic community and surrounding other brain types that went undiagnosed or undetected for many years, is that a person who grows up undiagnosed autistic, ADHD, OCD, etc. (usually co-occurring with other diagnoses whether it be mental illnesses or physical illnesses) doesn't have to look far to experience trauma.

This current conceptualization of root cause is believed to be the lack of accommodation, education and understanding that exists within the home, work/school and community environments around other typed brains and all which that encompasses.

What this all means is not only should neurodiverse individuals be approached with the understanding that they receive and deliver information differently, but that there is a statistically relevant probability that the individual you are interacting with has lived experience of a trauma element as well. This can show up as someone being less trusting, expressing communication worry, having overly extreme caution around socialization, or overexplaining themselves as they fear their words will be misrepresented or used out of context.

Many times, as therapists, we find ourselves working with neurodivergent youth and adolescents specifically, who have experienced trauma caused by more than just a systemic issue. Whether their trauma is a result of undiagnosed autism, or this is trauma surrounding the fact that an individual was undiagnosed as a child, which resulted in that person growing up navigating a neurotypical world without the knowledge of their brain type.

It is very probable that at the same time as everything else that was mentioned above that individuals are also struggling with other life trauma that doesn't directly have to do with a diagnosis of your brain type or other mental illness. However, no matter the origin or type of trauma that a person carries with them, it adds elements of difficulty, not only for the individual (this goes without saying), but the family and team members as well.

At this point, it is so important for the team of school professionals to be well trained in trauma informed care and support, so they can be a great ally and advocate for the individual for the duration of their participation on their student's team.

A great example of why training like that can be so important is our case study from this chapter. He had endured physical abuse before coming to live in his current safe situation. For this specific case, it was imperative that we worked with the school on creating scripts, rules and social stories for the student around when a new person would be coming to the school or classroom, what is a safe person, how to identify a safe person, and what the client can do if he didn't feel safe around someone. Who could he go to if he didn't feel safe around someone and who does he identify as a safe person within his school currently.

As a clinical team, we felt it was imperative to his growth, healing, and future safety that he felt safe enough in his school environment to not only learn this information but apply it. School is a place where new faces come and go consistently, learning how to use these skills and tools in that environment is a major key.

Knowing a student's background, especially in situations like this one, is so important. Not only is there a need to acknowledge the different brain type due to differences with how information is taken in, processed, and outsourced, but he also sees the world through a trauma lens. Trauma affects the brain's operating systems and similar ways to other neurodivergent brain types and it needs to be understood by all the professionals of the team you're working with

A large takeaway that academic teams could benefit from with a student comparable to the case study, is that when the student walks through the school doors, their trauma lens is never something that "shuts off."

There are much more in-depth details and information that are needed to come from a trauma informed perspective while working with any individual, let alone adding a divergent brain type. Unfortunately, in this framework, I don't have the ability to dive into this as a main subject to truly and thoroughly undertake it, which is the highlight it requires.

To provide due diligence, listed below are some affirming and ethical resources that may be helpful if you are looking for more skills, training and application.

1. https://www.kelly-mahler.com/resources/blog/unsafe-unheard-misunderstood-trauma-neurodiversity/

2. https://neurodiversity-training.therapistndc.org/product/neurodiversity-affirming-ethical-trauma-therapy/

3. https://catalog.pesi.com/item/a-neurodiversityaffirming-approach-treat-autistic-trauma-141962

Bringing It All Together

Key Takeaways

- Neurodiversity is not linear, and combinations of diagnoses always create complex needs and brain types.

- Being trauma informed any time you work with someone who holds history of trauma is extremely important.

- Understanding a student's history is very important.

- Tools like trainings for teachers and social stories for students can be used to enhance the student's progress and school experience.

Everyday Impact

- **For Parents:** You can also become trauma informed and it can be very helpful when working with your children and knowing how to advocate for their needs.

- **For Educators:** There is a chance that attempting interventions without being trauma informed can cause damage.

- **For Neurodivergent Adults:** Finding a trauma informed therapist or boss can be very important in protecting your own peace.

Let's Reflect

- Do you think all neurodivergent individuals experience trauma?

- In what ways have you experienced trauma in your life? How has it made it difficult for you to go places or do things? Would having a trauma informed person at those things make it easier?

Chapter 13
Naturally Assessed

*"Think of it: a disability is usually defined
in terms of what is missing...But autism...is as much about
what is abundant as what is missing, as over-expression
of the very traits that make our species unique."*
— Paul Collins (Author, Professor, Father of Autistic Child)

Chapter Expectations

- Become informed about Autism assessments

- Understand difference between affirming and medical model testing

- Assessments are not mandatory

When I first opened my private practice, it was truly out of personal desperation. My kids were young, undiagnosed, and unbeknownst to me, I was undiagnosed. I was drowning.

I was working as a super new, right out of graduate school, therapist at an associate's group practice and there wasn't enough time in my day to work, make enough money to support my family, take my kids through their diagnostic processes, OT, PT, pediatric psychiatry, take care of my own declining health, and support my husband, who was navigating his own mental health diagnoses at that time. There wasn't enough of me to go around, and I was on the verge of another autistic burnout.

With the support of some pretty awesome individuals in our mental health community here, I took a giant leap of faith and went into private practice. It was terrifying to say the least, but it was the best decision I ever made.

Within a few months, I was able to get my kids into the correct specialists to help them, and eventually we began to rebuild our home life and regain the strengths it needed to regain its baseline.

We found our new normal at home, and this allowed me to find myself, decide the kind of therapist I wanted to be, and begin building a therapy practice that had passion and purpose. As I became a specialist in my kid's information surrounding their autism diagnoses, I discovered my own autism diagnosis through theirs, as we do. Throughout this time, it became a therapeutic passion of mine, as we do, as well.

Yes, I became the most autistic, autistic person where not only did I research autism to the ends of the earth, but I also got multiple certifications in it, including now holding a Board Certification. Thus began my journey of rigorous training and practice to be able to provide neuro-affirming autism assessments for pediatric children, youth, adolescents, and adults.

Now, there is a lot of division over who professionally can provide these assessments. All I want to get into is that there are many amazing, therapeutic individuals that are able to provide these assessments legally that are also neuro-affirming and great at what they do, that are not psychologists, psychiatrists, or neurologists. I should also qualify that I am specifically writing this through Washington State Law and each state does need to specify what their state, county, and city laws, are and what your independent licensure laws are as well.

If you are a parent, teacher, administrator or any other person working with a child, and believe that the child is in need of some type of assessment, the first step is to discuss it with the person who can make an appointment with the child's main healthcare provider like a doctor or naturopath.

After that, once you have brought your concerns to them and discussed the possibility of an assessment, you can follow their suggestions. It is possible they want to have you begin with something like physical therapy or an action item having to do with a gastrointestinal need. You can then reach out to places around your area that provide neuropsychological assessments, or neuro-affirming autism assessments with differential diagnostics.

What's the difference you might ask? Well, let me tell you!

Neuropsychological evaluation is a diagnostic test that assesses your cognitive and emotional functioning. It uses standardized tests to measure how "well" the brain is functioning. The word "well" within this definition means that they are taking these scores and comparing them to data that are thought of to be milestones or benchmarks.

Not only does it look at your cognitive and emotional standings, but it also gets readings for social-emotional and academic function as well. This process goes through your attention, learning and memory, reasoning, language, mood, problem-solving skills, and more. Despite the extreme thoroughness of the neuropsychological evaluations, we are seeing many children and adults "fail" these evaluations and come away without any Autism or ADHD diagnosis despite it seeming more obvious that they are, in fact, operating with an Autistic/ADHD brain type.

The reasoning for why this is happening so frequently is mostly speculation at this point, but Dr. Russell Barkley, a Neuropsychologist and researcher, states that sole reliance on these tests has potential limitations, such as validity due to the test not reflecting real-world functionality. He also discusses that many false negatives result in these evaluations as they cannot account for masking or camouflaging as well as complex situations where they may score in the test for severe depression, but it cannot decipher between the symptoms someone is experiencing with their depression and ADHD.

I want to be clear that I am not, in any way, saying that neuropsychological evaluations should be avoided. These evaluations have their place and purpose and hold validity for individuals, and there are various scenarios in which they are sufficient, and will continue to be a main resource for many facets of assessments.

What I do want to point out, however, is this type of evaluation is strict in its delivery and doesn't have much room for any accommodation or change that an individual may need.

As pointed out by Dr. Russell Barkley earlier, at its baseline the neuropsychological evaluation doesn't have space for assessing the masking behaviors of individuals which can lead to an assessor perceiving someone completing the tasks within a "normal" range. This can provide invalidating results for individuals and lead to feelings of hopelessness and confusion. This is when it could be important for a person to take a self-report of something like the Camouflaging Autistic Traits Questionnaire (CAT-Q) to see how much of their day is dedicated to camouflaging strategies and in what situations they appear to use them most frequently.

Bottom line: I don't want any autistic person or other divergent typed individual to be invalidated or told they don't have a measurable diagnosis by an assessor just because they go to their assessment and make eye contact, hold a conversation, scored too "normal" on an assessment or choose not to fidget in the assessor's expected way.

Before we go any further, I think it is important to address another "elephant in the room." What makes me, an AuDHD individual, someone capable of assessing you when I am disabled myself.

It is important to bring this up as having an open dialogue around disability and stigmas around it is important. Don't worry, I'll help with how to begin the dialogue as I know it can be awkward to start and you're always taught not to ask about someone else's disability.

This is a question I get quite often. It's without fail that I will get asked what makes me someone that they, a client, should see over another clinician.

For the longest time I truly didn't know how to answer this question. In a field like mine, that is ever-growing and constantly collecting information, it's hard to define what an "expert" is, and I find it important to tread lightly when calling yourself one.

As long as you acknowledge that this field is ever changing and even as an expert you will still be continuously learning as you keep up with new information and training, I believe that counts as due diligence. We will never know everything; but you are a safe clinician in my book if you subscribe to the definition of expert as I do. Big bonus if you also realize a true expert knows you also learn just as much from a client as they learn from you.

However, all of these qualifications aside, something that really helped me with this concept, and for lack of a better term, marketing myself, was an excerpt from the book, Every Patient Tells A Story by Dr. Lisa Sanders.

The chapter I am referring to discussed her experience during the time she was shadowing Dr. Stanely Wainapel. This doctor became blind during his career, knowing from a young age that this would eventually be his fate. He had explained to the author, Dr. Sanders, that his disability ended up making him a better doctor than he was when he could see, because he had to rely on his patients' reports, their details, and his physical examination to be the best provider, and not be deceived by his eyes.

Later, in a discussion between the two doctors, she recounts in her book that he explained he never wanted his disability to handicap him and that he wanted people to see him as a doctor who happened to be blind, rather than letting it interfere with the services he could provide.

In listening to this, it hit me that I wanted to get the point across to my community and the population I served that being AuDHD did, in fact, make me a better clinician for my clients. It provided me with insight as well as lived experience I would never be able to learn from training or a textbook.

Of course, not every client and I will have had the exact experiences, but it can still provide clients with validation and language for things they may not have been able to get elsewhere. This is truly a unique skill I can offer and happily will do so. I never want my disabilities to make someone feel like it gets in the way of how I would be able to help them.

There is still a lot of taboo among other providers in the mental health and clinical field, where if you disclose your own diagnoses, clients will discount your ability to serve them. Now, I will tell you that there will be people who will in fact feel that way, and there is nothing anyone can say or do to change that. They believe, because of the provider's disabilities or diagnoses, that they are not properly fit to serve them.

If you are a disabled person who has decided to choose a profession in helping others, you are to be treasured and not discounted or torn apart. If that is you, and you are reading this, please know I am here rooting for you, cheering for you and proud of all that you have accomplished. As Nicki Minaj so unapologetically raps in her song Side to Side with Ariana Grande "I give zero f*c*s, and I got zero chill in me".

I am proud to say that I am an autistic voice that can help others like me, and I never view it as a deficit. This is something that I want to carry through in my work as a clinician, parent, and advocate.

We are very lucky in the region where I live as there are many providers who give neuro-affirming autism evaluations and neuropsychological evaluations, and I was able to be at the receiving end of one of them myself. Our area is not perfect by any means, but we are far better off when it comes to resources than many others.

Traditional vs. Neuro-Affirming Assessment Approaches

Below is a breakdown of some of the main differences between a traditional assessment and a neuro-affirming assessment. Please keep in mind that these are general differences and each assessor may have different steps that they take throughout their assessment process.

Gender Understanding
Traditional: Outdated info around gender stereotypes

Neuro-Affirming: Gender-fluid information is included and respected

View on Social Dynamics
Traditional: Assumes autistic individuals aren't interested in social dynamics
Neuro-Affirming: Recognizes both external and internal social dynamics and relies on self-reported experiences

Assessment Structure
Traditional: Maintains strict instructions during assessment
Neuro-Affirming: Offers accommodations to make the individual comfortable during assessment

Information Acceptance
Traditional: Only accepts data that fits the assessment protocol
Neuro-Affirming: Accepts all information provided by the individual and considers it valid during diagnosis

Behavioral Focus
Traditional: Focuses on behaviors such as eye contact, conversation skills, and ability to maintain a job
Neuro-Affirming: Screens for masking behaviors (e.g., faking eye contact, conversation scripting, sensory sensitivities)

Diagnostic Model
Traditional: Uses a medical model and compares to a neurotypical baseline
Neuro-Affirming: Identifies traits that describe a brain style or type without comparison to a "norm"

Terminology and Framing
Traditional: Identifies "deficits" and "impairments"
Neuro-Affirming: Uses a strengths-based lens and focuses on unmet needs

Post-Assessment Recommendations
Traditional: Makes generic recommendations based on a

generalized neurodivergent profile
Neuro-Affirming: Suggests tailored strategies, accommodations, and supports based on individual needs

Emotional Impact
Traditional: Can feel invalidating or dismissive, even if a diagnosis is given
Neuro-Affirming: Helps individuals feel understood and heard, fostering a sense of individualized care

Diagnostic Accuracy
Traditional: Individuals may walk away undiagnosed despite qualifying, due to outdated or rigid assessment models
Neuro-Affirming: Provides validation and explanation for masking behaviors, increasing diagnostic clarity

When it comes time for an assessment, whether you are looking for an assessment as an adult and you're seeking a diagnosis later in life, or you are a parent looking for an assessment for your child, the most important part is having the knowledge to navigate the process.

The services that are available can be difficult to find and navigate. Understanding where to start can be hard and if you find yourself with little to no support, it can be daunting. There can be many times where you can find yourself led in the wrong direction and discouraged. Knowing the difference between a traditional assessment and a neuro-affirming assessment is one of the first important pieces of information to have.

Deciding to get an assessment is a personal choice and whether you are self-diagnosed or diagnosed by a professional, your diagnosis is valid.

Bringing It All Together

Key Takeaways

- Self-diagnosis is valid and assessments can be hard to obtain.

- Differences in assessments can sometimes mean the difference between getting a diagnosis or not.

- Assessments that speak to a person's deficits can be invalidating.

- There isn't one way to be autistic or any other diagnosis, so the assessments should not be looking for that either.

Everyday Impact

- **For Parents:** You may have to spend some time finding an assessor that is a good fit.

- **For Educators:** Creating a relationship with an assessor in the community that you see putting students first can be a huge help to parents.

- **For Neurodivergent Adults:** If you are self-diagnosed the only reason to get an assessment is if you need services or accommodations.

Let's Reflect

- Have you suspected your child to be autistic? Have you thought you may be autistic yourself? What first made you suspect this?

- How might you go about looking for resources in your community?

Chapter 14
Naturally Proficient

"It is easier to build strong children
than to repair broken men [people]."
– Fredrick Douglass (Activist, Author, Abolitionist)

Chapter Expectations

- What it looks like to be an expert in your home

- Why parents find themselves in expert roles

- Community resources and availability

Normally I begin each chapter with a client case study, but for this chapter, it will be approached from more of a generalized case study and something that so many people find themselves working through.

There is a systemic issue when it comes to the healthcare system as a whole and much of it is outside of our control. Despite the inability to have control over the entire system, it is still important to have open conversations about the feelings, struggles and strategies that surround it.

Any time parents come through my office to discuss their needs, they always thank me for the strategies and information I provide them with. However, I think it is always important to remind them of one major thing; you as parents are truly the expert on your child. You may not be the expert on what they are going through or what they are experiencing mentally or physically, but you are most definitely the expert on your child.

This concept is very important for this chapter as we begin to talk about what it means to become an expert in a topic surrounding your child and why we have to become that expert as parents. Just as it is stated in previous chapters, seeking help doesn't mean you have failed your child, and asking for tools or strategies doesn't mean you have done anything wrong leading up to that moment.

Important question.

What do we do when we come up against something and don't know much about it?

Many of us may answer this question differently as I am sure we all have different tools in our toolbox, but what I can say for myself is that I begin researching. Now, before you begin picturing me like that meme of Charlie Day where he has a subject board covered in documents, and a giant red string connecting key concepts and he is attempting to explain it, notably with very little sleep, I promise I begin with a healthy amount of research; most of the time.

Once that has been completed and I have acquainted myself with the material, I will look around to see what resources I can access based on the information I found. Unfortunately, this is the point where many of us realize that there aren't resources or they have managed to become unreachable.

For parents, teachers, and other professionals, this happens more often than not. Whether they don't have the support, they don't possess the funding, or they have been put on a three year waitlist, any resources they may be finding are difficult to access. Many struggle to have access to support or information needed to know what the best move would be through their new situation, and they feel inadequate to navigate alone.

A personal instance of this was when my child was diagnosed with pediatric bipolar under the age of 10. The rate of a bipolar diagnosis in adults at this time in our world is statistically not uncommon, at 1 in 150 people (WHO, 2024).

Now, if we are to discuss pediatric bipolar, which consists of ages 5-9, the statistics currently calculate its rate at 27 in 100,000 children (NLM, 2021).

This shows that the diagnosis for pediatrics is far more uncommon and as I did my research to find help, the resources were just as rare as the diagnosis. By the time of his diagnosis, our home and child were enduring many manic and depressive episodes as well as rapid cycling daily. At this point we all felt desperate.

At this point, like many parents and professionals in similar situations, I felt stuck and hopeless. It was becoming abundantly clear that the resources were not there and if I wanted to get anywhere, I was going to have to do it myself. So thus began my deep, deep dive into the world of pediatric mood disorders, and bipolar. Hours upon hours of clinical trainings and books of information; I was drilling it all into my head. I finally gained the knowledge I was craving, and the support that I needed.

This is where it is important to call out this brutal and unfair cycle. Yes, I am a mental health professional, but at home I am still just a parent. No parent should have to take on clock hours and continuing education courses just to learn how to support their child's needs due to a failure of systems and a resource desert.

This is a point where parents, caregivers, teachers and other professionals who are in need of support and are simply looking for information during their greatest time of need, and they are left with the message that they must be their own therapist, doctor, coach, and mentor.

Time and time again, people experiencing some of life's greatest struggles find themselves up against the largest barriers. My current working theory behind this is the help that is needed requires a lot of effort and work, and it can be hard to base a niche career off things that are less likely to happen to someone.

So, here I am, writing this book with a new certification in pediatric mood disorders and bipolar disorders and I have been able to understand and help my own child much better.

I have the proper language and understanding to report back to and discuss unmet needs with his psychiatrist, and he is now getting better care. Not because the psychiatrist was ever doing anything wrong, truth be told, as we were lucky to have found an amazing psychiatrist to join our family team. It was because before my learning, I didn't have the right knowledge, understanding or language to report correctly to her and to receive the correct help for my child.

I find it astounding how many parents email me or inquire for help and they have already gathered the language to ask for help. I understand that they are most likely in a similar position and did the same thing I did for my child. These families recognize signs they are drowning at home or are struggling with a certain aspect of their child's needs, possibly their own, and they begin researching and collecting information, eventually making it to me.

By doing this, many families do a wonderful job describing their needs and what is going on in their home. What I find sad is that we don't have the feeling of security to not research much of anything or not second-guess ourselves, and just go to the specialists and allow them to do the hard work for us.

Aside from there being a lack of support for finding resources, there is also the difficult task of filtering through all the information that someone may find during their research time. For instance, information that is found on Autism is primarily reported from studies that compile data from boys and boys who have externally presenting profiles. That means that this information is not helpful for anyone outside of these categories, and could convince someone they are on the wrong path.

Something that perpetuates this cycle is that when this profile stereotype continues to be highlighted as the only main presentation of Autism, in educational trainings, media representation and in books. Due to this being current mainstream representation, even in places like doctor's offices, where educators, care staff, and other childcare workers are trained in, and only informed of, this presentation and nothing else.

When we talk about encouraging a neuro-affirming environment, it is also important to know that most people we are training have been doing the best they can with the information and resources they have. I say this due to the exact reasoning of many places only providing information or trainings based off of 10% of information.

Another factor of importance to note is how to navigate social media resources. A lot of our resources via social media are wonderful and have so many positive factors such as finding a specialist, support from other parents or home resources. Make sure that you are cautious of people that you meet online or reach out to you that may lead you in the wrong direction. A great example of this are Facebook support groups. As much as social media support groups can be great for various reasons, there can be a downside as well.

Within these support groups, there isn't anyone validating the advice with mental or medical professionals. There can be situations where parents who may not have similar viewpoints or morals, may give incorrect or medically unsupported information or viewpoints, that can end up being invalidating for a neurodivergent person or can even lead down the road of incorrectly diagnosing a person. It is very important that no matter what leads you decide to follow, that you check the sources it comes from, and make sure that they are neuro-affirming in practice.

As parents, we really do it all.

We naturally become experts in anything our kids need, sometimes without protecting our own peace as parents. Remember, that as a parent, you deserve your own peace as well and your happiness is just as important as your child's. All the hard work that you've been putting in will have results, even if it doesn't feel like it today.

Tomorrow is a new day full of growth and possibilities, and nothing is too big to acquire help for.

Bringing It All Together

Key Takeaways

- This field is still growing in knowledge and providers.

- Finding specialist providers can be very difficult due to the newness of the field, and the needs of people.

- Just because it is difficult doesn't mean it is impossible, continue to seek support so you are not alone.

- You and your child are their expert, and what you are experiencing is imposter syndrome.

Everyday Impact

- **For Parents:** When it gets hard, reach out for support from your community or support system.

- **For Educators:** You can be such a valuable ally for families and a large key in helping with reporting once specialists are found.

- **For Neurodivergent Adults:** You are an expert on you! If you find a provider telling you otherwise, remember they work for you and let them know you will be finding a new one!

Let's Reflect

- Who is currently part of your support system? Do you feel supported by them? What are some things you need support with right now?

- Have you been leaning into a topic lately that you have needed to be an expert in for yourself or someone in your family?

Chapter 15
Naturally Feminine

"It makes it very hard to work out where you belong when you are brilliant at things that others find hard, but useless at things that others find easy."
– Sarah Hendrickx (Clinician, Author)

Chapter Expectations

- Learn about misdiagnosing/no diagnosis for autism with female born individuals

- Understand challenges these individuals come up against

- Gain knowledge around female (or other) less known autism traits

Every autistic female who has come through my office for an assessment has said the same thing. They have been turned away, overlooked or told they were not autistic because they were "too pretty", "they made eye contact", "they were too smart" or "they held a conversation."

To answer the question that just popped into your brain: yes, these are all real quotes; yes, they're from real people; yes, they were licensed professionals; and yes, these are actual clinical statements explaining some of the reasons people were denied a diagnosis. Yikes—I know, right?!

It is disappointing to know that so many of these people went to seek help and were invalidated by licensed providers whom these individuals were trying to get validation and salvation through.

Unfortunately, each girl, woman and female born person would tell me the same thing and not only was it hard as I sat there hearing their stories, watching their hurt and desperation pour from their body, but it hits home with me as I went through my own batter's line up of professionals who all told me similar things as to why there was clearly "nothing wrong with me."

My usual response to those professionals who would say that was that I actually agreed with them, and that I also thought there was nothing wrong with me and I just simply thought I was Autistic, but that never seemed to go over well either.

As females, the "official" diagnostic numbers may be lower, but the numbers still speak volumes. The rate of autistic females to autistic males reported in 2022 was 1:3 and in 2022 it was reported that women were two times more likely to die by suicide than men (NAMI, 2023).

I will just let you sit with that one for a minute.

Autism studies, information and assessments originated with white men and unfortunately provided a very small group of traits, data and criteria. It also has some other dark origins and although I do love a good origin story as you know, this one isn't my favorite.

Due to the content of this specific history lesson, I will leave it up to each reader to decide how much of a deep dive you want to take into that on your own time. Despite the incredible research and progress in the field over the past seven years—expanding diagnostic criteria across different genders, races, ethnicities, comorbidities, and ages—our American Diagnostic Criteria have not made much progress.

Instead, it depends on each individual provider, what they are willing to educate themselves on, and what they find to be essential to Autism diagnostics. Hopefully, in the next DSM addition we will see more widespread criteria that lean towards the light of inclusiveness and embrace the true spectrum of Autism.

The idea is that it would validate all human presentation of Autism and make it easier when it came to identifying each individual. An important result that would come from this change is education opportunities created for populations who work with children.

Due to the lack of information, many females and late-diagnosed autistics, have been publishing their own clinical work and narratives in order to help others find their own way through this process.

Examples of some of these brave individuals are Dr. Emilia Misheva, Paige Layle, and Bianca Toeps. They discuss research and anecdotes, but a common thread brought up is continuous confusion around females and empathy during the diagnostic process.

Contrary to stereotypical beliefs that have been brought forth by the myths discussed surrounding autism, such as that autistic people do not possess empathy, assessors sometimes find it confusing when they are assessing someone and the person describes emotions, or they are empathetic towards the assessor.

However, it is actually very common, specifically more common in female autistic individuals, to show empathy towards inanimate objects such as a stuffed animal or a rock. This could look like a person getting a new stuffed animal, introducing it to the stuffed animals currently in their room, and then making sure it has space on their bed for the night. They may also feel guilty later as they wonder if these actions made any of the other stuffed animals feel sad or left out.

Another example of this extreme empathy that can be felt is that a person may feel an overwhelming sense of empathy for world hunger and go to the extent of not eating so as to be in solidarity with those people. This type of emotion can be quite a big deal as it can bring on their feelings of empathy but also fit into a category of their strong sense of justice.

I can say, personally, I had a giant collection of Beanie Babies as a kid and teen. I'm sure you'd all be shocked to hear I was a '90s kid—and there were many times I wondered if they felt neglected as I kept collecting more and more.

As I got older, I began to wonder if I was projecting those feelings onto them so I wouldn't have to acknowledge my own guilt—that I was spending so much money in pursuit of something selfish, growing a collection that didn't hold any real value to the world, instead of using that money to make a more meaningful impact.

Yeah, talk about a chill Friday night topic to discuss with your friends over pizza and ice cream. See, guys? I didn't need that counselor the substitute was talking about... I totally did!

Below I have provided a table of traits that may help someone identify Autism in a female born person. Remember that they still may not fall exactly into these traits, because as humans we are not checklists.

A person and their brain will always have exceptions or not fall into an exact stereotypical behavior that someone else has experienced despite it being the case a majority of the time; this is why assessments are always necessary and so important.

This is why flexibility, and a deep understanding of the diagnosis are key when doing an assessment for someone.

Assessment-Named Behaviors in Autistic Females and Masking Patterns

Below are common behaviors noted during assessments, how they may present in autistic females, and how masking behaviors may influence or obscure them.

Behavior: Eye Contact

Autistic Female Behavior:

- May make eye contact when talking, look away when thinking

- Looks at people in other areas of the face

Masking Behavior:

- May make eye contact intentionally.
  (*To assess masking, ask how they feel about eye contact and check for true conversation comprehension.*)

Behavior: Social Communication

Autistic Female Behavior:

- Overly social

- Will talk to anyone and shows no stranger anxiety or worry

Masking Behavior:

- May communicate despite not wanting to, as a social survival strategy

Behavior: Repetitive Behaviors

Autistic Female Behavior:

- Biting inside of the lip

- Biting nails

- Picking fingers

- Leg bouncing

Masking Behavior:

- These are often seen as socially acceptable behaviors and can be missed due to neurotypical assessor bias

Behavior: Social Play

Autistic Female Behavior:

- Takes a leading or instructive role

- Appears to engage in free play, but often reenacts scenes or structures from other contexts

Masking Behavior:

- This is often perceived as socially appropriate "play" and can lead to the child being seen as "non-autistic"

Behavior: Emotional Presentation

Autistic Female Behavior:

- Can score across the Empathy-to-Alexithymia spectrum

- May show extreme empathy

- May be unaware of others' emotions or their own

Masking Behavior:

- Learns emotional "rules" to survive social interactions

- Uses rehearsed emotional responses during assessments

It is important to remember that there is no correct way to be an autistic female, there isn't a correct way to be an autistic male, and we need to remember as clinicians, teachers and professionals, we must assess that way as well.

When being in the role of a professional, you may be the gateway to services, and it's important to not close those doors for someone based on a stereotype that is proven to be false time and time again. To make sure these mistakes don't happen, communication and connection are key.

Bringing in the family and other team members is important, and referring to other specialists when it is out of your scope of practice is a requirement, and not a suggestion.

Bringing It All Together

Key Takeaways

- If you are autistic, there is nothing wrong with you, however, you are still entitled to seek out help.

- Female born individuals have a significantly harder time receiving a diagnosis than men.

- At this point, it shouldn't be hard to get help, places are not keeping up with new research and information.

- Information here can help you ask the right questions in seeking out the right fit in an assessor for you.

Everyday Impact

- **For Parents:** Express to assessors when you don't like how something is going, or you don't agree with the results.

- **For Educators:** Bringing this information to them could help them avoid frustration and misdiagnosis for their child.

- **For Neurodivergent Adults:** Hopefully this information can help you avoid going through the same struggles I did.

Let's Reflect

- Think of a time when you had a doctor's appointment that felt uncomfortable? How did you feel after? How did you handle it?

- How might this chapter change the way you seek out assessment services or any other services in the future?

Conclusion
Naturally Concluded

I am someone who was never good at goodbyes and even found them awkward. I always struggled with how to handle the other person's emotions and therefore began to not like them. I know this is all pretty priceless coming from a therapist.

I still leave the very minimal parties I attend without saying farewell, and will quietly slip out the door without anyone noticing. I will find a way to leave for a trip without a goodbye, but rather leave on the note of a good conversation and a fantastic meal, without acknowledging the ending of the time together with the person.

I may make a comment on how I will contact them, but I won't acknowledge the finality of what is to come.

When someone leaves a session from my office or my kids leave the house, I say "see you soon," or murmur something along the lines of "have a good rest of your day."

I don't like the idea of goodbyes; it really is the finality of it. I don't like the idea of telling someone that they may not see me again, because in my brain I am already envisioning the next time I see them and how I will approach it.

So, just like I would in any other place in my life, I am going to end this book without saying goodbye.

I am going to say that this is the end of this book, because I feel that I have concluded the main ideas that I was hoping to provide to you as readers.

You have been given the proper amount of information to begin laying a foundation of neuro-affirming environments for the neurodivergent people around you. You should now be able to communicate and connect better with those in your life that are not neurotypical, as well as empathize with the journey that they have been through to get to where they are today.

I am proud of you for making it all the way to the end of this book and as Grover said in his famous book, There is a Monster At the end of this Book, "Well, look at that! This is the end of the book, and the only one here is...Me."

Now, why is this important, you may ask?

This is important because the only one tracking your progress is you, the only one who knows that you're putting in the work is you, and the only one who can continue to make this place better and more neuro-affirming is you!

Thank you for taking time out of your life to read what I had to say, and hopefully, together we can continue to make this place safer for everyone.

So... See you soon, and have a great day!

Appendix

Table of Contents

Appendix I
TERMS glossary

504: This is a formal plan designed to document the accommodation and modifications a student needs to have access to their educational setting. This is something that can help a student have equal access to academics and other school activities such as PE, music and field trips. The Rehabilitation Act of 1973, which is a federal civil rights law, prohibits any discrimination based on disability.

AAC: Augmentative and Alternative Communication devices are tools that assist individuals with speech-language communication. These are devices that are designed to be used by a variety of people and assisting different needs; it's also wonderful for people of all ages. They can be classified into three categories: High-tech, Mid-tech, and Low-tech. Some examples of these devices are: speech-generating devices, eye gaze systems, iPads, and communication boards.

ADHD: Attention-Deficit/Hyperactivity Disorder is a neurodevelopmental brain difference that is characterized by persistent patterns of inattention, hyperactivity, and impulsivity that interfere with a person's ability to confidently complete daily tasks or achieve neurotypical development and social expectations. ADHD has many different presentations and should not be classified based on its stereotypical presentation in young males such as "the energizer bunny" profile, or the "never sticks with one thing" trope.

Antecedent: A preceding event, condition, or cause of a behavior.

AuDHD: Autism + ADHD is its own brain type and has been proven to have a different functioning type.

Body Doubling: A practice where someone does boring, difficult, or frustrating tasks in the presence of another person.

DSM-5: The Diagnostic and Statistical Manual of Mental Disorders, Fifth Edition: A handbook that provides a common language for diagnosing and classifying mental disorders. This is used by clinicians, researchers, and public health officials to diagnose mental disorders and psychiatric illnesses. This manual includes descriptions, symptoms and other criteria for diagnosing, and guidance for making objective assessments of symptom presentation. The most updated version is the DSM-5TR and it was published in March 2022. It was the revision of The DSM-5 that was published in 2013.

IEP: Individualized Education Plan is a legal document that describes and outlines a student's specific education services, supports and academic, social and emotional goals. This is a document that is created based on a collaboration by a team of professionals that contributes to the student's needs, including (but not limited to) parents, teachers, medical specialists, and therapists to make sure the student is receiving a holistic approach.

Neuro-Affirming: The philosophy of neurodivergent brain types being embraced as valid, equal and never in need of repair. This is a strength-based approach that celebrates individuality.

Neurodivergent: People who have brain types that fall outside of the societal "norm." This is an umbrella term and includes a massive range of diagnoses and brain types.

Neurodiversity: Idea that there is a natural variation in the way that brains work, including all humans.

Neurotypical: People who have a brain type that falls within the societal "norm."

PDA: Pathological Demand Avoidance or Persistent Drive for Autonomy. This is a profile of Autism Spectrum Disorder and is part of their core characteristics. Unfortunately, despite the research, understanding and evidence-based practices that already exist, America still currently doesn't acknowledge this as a diagnosis or anxiety profile. You will find it acknowledged again, by those neuro-affirming providers. PDA is best described as the person experiencing a fight, flight, freeze, or fawn, response when faced with demands that their body biologically deems to be a threat to their autonomy.

PECS: Picture Exchange Communication System is a very specific type of communication device. It was developed in 1985, and it is specific pictures that represent words that can be used in multiple ways for communication.

Self-Diagnose: The act of diagnosing yourself because you strongly align with the criteria for the diagnosis. For neurodivergent people this usually happens after taking multiple self-report scale assessments online, watching content from other neurodivergent individuals, and doing a large amount of research. Due to an issue with resources and capability of obtaining an assessment in our medical system, self-diagnosis is seen as valid by many neuro-affirming providers. This is especially the case when looking at Autism Spectrum Disorder.

SPD: Sensory Processing Disorder, formally known as sensory integration dysfunction, is a condition where multisensory input is not adequately processed by a person in order to provide appropriate responses for themselves based on the demands of the environment. It can also mean that an individual has difficulty detecting, modulating, interpreting, and/or responding to any sensory experience. Their brain can struggle to process sensory information from things such as sights, sounds, smells movement, and touch.

WHO: World Health Organization, founded in 1948. They are the United Nations agency that connects nations, partners and people to promote health, keep the world safe and serve the vulnerable – so everyone, everywhere can attain the highest level of health (Direct from the WHO website).

Appendix II

Possible Accommodation Ideas for Your Student

- Preferred seating

- Preferred class schedule and the ability to change classes if needed

- Preferred teacher for various reasons

- Unlimited access to the bathroom, food, and water

- All materials and directions provided in both a visual and written form

- Access to a break when needed; examples of a break could be Legos, coloring, or reading. The location of the break is dependent on the child

- Access to sensory space

- Access to an isolation space (this is a space that they go to by choice, not one they are forced into or is used as a punishment)

- Access to a change of clothing—have clothing sent from home and available at school

- Access to a mobility break —this can look many ways. Make sure to consult with an occupational therapist or physical therapist; these services are available at most schools.

- Access to a low stimulus classroom —This can look like having a specific classroom set up that follows the rules of calm colors, decrease in 'visual noise', less clutter, clearly marked items, own items marked with black/white

- Having a reader

- Access to speech-to-text or a scribe

- Create pre-written sentences for someone to complete if they cannot generate ideas for free writing

- Communication devices

- First-Then prompts

- Task Breakdown

- Organizers

- Visual Schedule

- Doing things in repetition

Appendix III
Literature Resources

- **Navigating PDA in America** — Ruth Fidler and Diane Gould

- **But You Don't Look Autistic at All** — Bianca Toeps

- **Magnificent Minds** — Suzanne Goh, MD

- **Gifted and Distractable** — Julie F. Skolnick

- **Unmasking Autism** — Devon Price, PhD

- **Unlearning Shame** — Devon Price, PhD

- **Brain-Body Parenting** — Mona Delahooke

- **The Reason I Jump** — Naoki Higashida

- **The Neuroscience of You** — Chantel Prat, PhD

- **Under the Radar** — Dr. Emilia Misheva

- **Nurturing Your Autistic Young Person** — Cathy Wassell

- **The Bipolar Child** — Demitri Papolos, MD, and Janice Papolos

- **The Anti-Ableist Manifesto** — Tiffany Yu

- **All Tangled Up in Autism and Chronic Illness** — Charli Clement

- **Raising Trans Kids** — Rebecca Minor

- **Queerly Autistic** — Erin Ekins

Appendix IV
Communication Form Example

Name:

I Don't Like:

It is hard because:

Something I want you to know:

What I need right now:

Do I need a break?:

Appendix VI
Works Cited

1. https://pmc.ncbi.nlm.nih.gov/articles/PMC6997554/#:~:text=About%2090%25%20of%20ASD%20individuals,representing%20a%20very%20frequent%20finding (NCBI, 2020).

2. https://www.who.int/news-room/fact-sheets/detail/mental-health-strengthening-our-response (WHO, 2023).

3. https://health.ucdavis.edu/news/headlines/autism-characteristics-can-change-significantly-from-ages-3-to-11/2022/04#:~:text=Waizbard%2DBartov:%20There%20are%20many,getting%20the%20intervention%20they%20need. (UC DAVIS, 2022).

4. https://pmc.ncbi.nlm.nih.gov/articles/PMC8233426/#:~:text=For%20example%3A%20In%20the%205,2015). (NLM, 2021).

5. https://pmc.ncbi.nlm.nih.gov/articles/PMC7139720/#:~:text=Studies%20have%20revealed%20that%20the,55%2C56%2C57%5D (NCBI, 2020.1).

6. https://pmc.ncbi.nlm.nih.gov/articles/PMC11042491/ (NAMI, 2023).

7. Every Patient Tells a Story By: Dr. Lisa Sanders, 2009

8. The Anti-Ableist Manifesto By: Tiffany Yu, 2024

9. Navigating PDA in America By: Ruth Fidler and Diane Gould, 2024

10. Under the Radar By: Dr. Emilia Misheva, 2024

About the author

Calial McCarty, MA, LMHC, CAS, is an AuDHD mental health therapist and a passionate advocate for neuro-affirming care.

Holding a Master of Arts in Mental Health and Wellness and School Counseling K-12 from New York University (2020) and a Bachelor of Science in Behavioral Science of Psychology in Applied Behavior Analysis from Purdue University Global (2018), she is a Washington state licensed clinician and a Board Certified Autism Specialist. She is also an Active ADOS-2 Administrator and MIGDAS Administrator.

Throughout her career, Calial has worked extensively with community agencies, courts, schools, and various mental health programs. She specializes in behavior analysis, developmental disabilities, co-occurring disorders, and trauma-informed psychotherapy for individuals ages 0-17 years and their families. In her eclectic approach, she deeply values client voice, safety, and self-advocacy, believing that art, play, and storytelling are fundamental modalities in the foundation of healing.

Naturally Divergent is Calial's first published book, born from her profound belief that children, youth, and families need more support than ever to rebuild their foundations and thrive.

When not immersed in her work, Calial enjoys exploring the world with her husband and children, reading, and traveling. She hopes this book will inspire readers to educate themselves, foster curiosity, and embrace diverse perspectives.

www.ingramcontent.com/pod-product-compliance
Lightning Source LLC
Chambersburg PA
CBHW060139150626
46550CB00015B/2152